I Ain't in Kansas *No More!*

This Can't be God....
It feels too real!!

Rev. Dr. Kenneth D. Linnell OSL

ISBN: 979-8-89031-592-2 (sc)
ISBN: 979-8-89031-593-9 (hc)
ISBN: 979-8-89031-594-6 (e)

Because of the dynamic nature of the Internet, any web addresses or links contained in this book may have changed since publication and may no longer be valid. The views expressed in this work are solely those of the author and do not necessarily reflect the views of the publisher, and the publisher hereby disclaims any responsibility for them.

One Galleria Blvd., Suite 1900, Metairie, LA 70001
(504) 702-6708

MARANATHA

[*]maranatha. This Aramaic word, which occurs at
I Cor. 16:22, was understood by the christian fathers as the
"the Lord has come", but it is probably more correctly rendered
by the imperative "O Lord, come" (cf. Rev. 22:20), Its use by
St. Paul reflects the strong eschatological hopes of the early Church

---

[*] pg. 1031-1032, the Oxford Dictionary of the Christian Church, edited by F.L.
Cross, Third Edition by E.A. Livingstone, Oxford university Press 1997

CONTENTS

PART I:
BEGINNINGS

PART II:
NO FRILLS NO THRILLS

DEDICATION

The number of persons to whom this work could be dedicated are numerous. However, there is only one who truly deserves this dedication. You will meet her in these pages, but truthfully that will only provide the reader with a mere glance at this truly remarkable woman. Therefore it is with love and a portion of humility for the life we have shared, I dedicate this work to:

Debbie,
my wife, my friend, and my lover.

When I began this work, as you might imagine, I had a title in mind, yet, as the writing progressed more and more titles presented themselves as possibilities. Also as the pages took shape it became apparent that rather than a simple telling of the birth of the Schooner Maranatha, this tale also of necessity, became a story of beginnings. My own as the oldest child of my parents, my own as a child of God. My life as Debbie was given to me, and that of the Maranatha herself, and of our lives with her.

As I wrote I was reminded of Dorthy in the Wizard of Oz and of her telling her little dog Toto, "we're not in Kansas any more."

The metaphor of Kansas in the story, to which Dorothy is constantly attempting to return, is that of her sanctuary, her safe place, home. The story is in may ways the story of Dorthy searching for a way to return to that safe place. In this brief telling of my life I came to realize that like

Dorothy, I have spent most of my life attempting to return to Kansas. Metaphorically, Kansas, is also my safe place, the sanctuary for which I searched most of my life.

In Dorothy's story a tornado took her from her safe place. The tornado in my story was my father's death in January 1945, from that moment my safe place ceased to be, and my life was instantly transported to a "Land of Oz." As I committed this portion of my story to print I came to realize, "I ain't in Kansas no more!"

All that is written here is true and portrayed as accurately as is humanly possible. Some of the things you read here might seem hard to believe, yet, they happened just as they are recorded. Many other stories of the life and times of the S/V Maranatha are not told here, out of consideration for space and time, however, they may some day find their way to the written page.

I hope you enjoy reading about our lives with the Maranatha as much as I have enjoyed writing them down, even though at times the memories are painful.

February 21, 2015
Rev. Dr. Kenneth D. Linnell OSL
Captain S/V Maranatha
The month of Adar

PROLOGUE

JANUARY 21, 1990, 0130 HOURS

The satellite navigation system finally came up with a good fix. It placed us approximately ninety miles south south east of Government Cut. The name of a rather nondescript opening in the sand, which cuts through the barrier island just south of Apalachicola, Florida. We had passed through this cut into the waters of the Gulf of Mexico some twelve hours earlier.

The S/V Maranatha was met by a twenty knot wind on her starboard bow and short choppy eight foot seas almost dead on her bow. Like a true lady of the sea, she made her curtsy to Neptune, dipping her bows into the seas as the first swells greeted and welcomed her to the openness of Neptune's domain. She had stuck her nose into the seas, healed over to the wind, and in these adverse conditions had averaged seven and a half knots of speed as she made her way through the seas. S/V Maranatha seemed to be enjoying the ride as we left the north coast of Florida behind.

It was tough going as the short scope of the seas caused by the relatively shallow waters of the Gulf, made for a hobby horse motion, with the bow rising high as it met the waves and the stern falling quickly as another wave met the bow even before the previous cycle could complete. The S/V Maranatha met them all as they came moving gracefully through the seas on this dark foggy January night in the northeastern Gulf of Mexico.

Maranatha was a world unto herself, rolling headlong into the fog and occasional rain, surrounded by a glow of red and green cast onto the fog by the vessels running lights. The faint white light of the mast head danced its way fifty foot above as the roll of the S/V Maranatha helped it to paint an arch across Maranatha's world surrounded by darkness, fog and agitated stormy seas.

Debbie and I were hunkered down, wrapped up in blankets, on the cockpit benches. Our two cats "Meow" and "Kitty Mac" were coiled up in tight furry balls alongside Debbie. All of S/V Maranatha's crew were attempting to stay warm and dry, but mostly losing the battle.

Debbie and I knew, as we sailed on through the night, that shortly we would pass one of those imaginary lines we humans have drawn around the earth, called lines of latitude. We knew as we passed below one of these lines of latitude, which not only bring "changes of attitude" as Jimmy Buffet sings, our journey would bring us into the tropical waters of south Florida. Thus bringing us into southern climes, warm water, and the warm sunny skies of the tropics.

Maranatha's radar, which represented almost a year's servitude on my part, clearly seeing through the dark and fog, illuminated any obstacles in our path. Gabriel, our auto pilot, six months servitude, busily took care of the helm, constantly adjusting for wind and seas keeping us on course for Tampa Bay, our first stop before heading for points south.

All that was remaining for me to do, beside staying warm and dry, was to keep a vigilant eye on the radar and make any course adjustments that might be required to miss any obstacles in our path. I also had to go below regularly to make safety checks and look at the navigation equipment to keep up on our position. I also maintained a dead reckoning plot across the chart. By doing this we could keep a reasonably certain knowledge of our position on the vast open landscape of dark rolling water. I should point out that our navigation system was what was known at the time a "Sat-Nav" not the now familiar "GPS". The Sat-Nav was a precursor of the GPS and at the time very up to date.

Its draw back was that there were only a very few satellites, resulting in long periods of no signal or fix. It required more or less constant monitoring when at sea for you never knew when a fix on your position would come through. Better then nothing, but just.

Debbie, an eternal victim to motion sickness, had at last given in to the never ending pitch and roll. She was mildly ill, that is, as observed by someone who has never suffered that particular form of torture. She was curled up on the starboard cockpit bench, holding out very well against that most ancient of sea god's "Ralph", so named for the sound one makes as they cast their "accounts" over board, while silently praying for the motion to mercifully end, or sudden death to occur, with no preference whatsoever as to which should occur first.

As "Captain", I was in my element, S/V Maranatha after long years of delay, construction and delay in other areas, was finally sailing through the sea firmly pointed into the mission for which she had been created.

S/V Maranatha was working well under jib, fore sail, and reefed main. The radar provided eyes in the darkness, and "Gabriel' was at the helm. All was right with S/V Maranatha and her crew.

We were on the second leg of a journey which was to take us from Pensacola, Florida to our mission field in the islands of the Caribbean, with a brief stop in Tampa, Florida to visit friends.

It was a journey delayed more than two years, since our arrival in Pensacola, following the birth of S/V Maranatha on a red Oklahoma hilltop, her excursion down the Arkansas and lower Mississippi rivers, and across the northern Gulf of Mexico to Pensacola.

These adventures are the impetus for the telling of this story. It is the tale of what can and sometimes does happen when a man decides to follow his God no matter what the rest of the world, more especially those who profess to be Christians, think of the call of God on a mans life. This is also the story of a woman who gives up everything through faith in her God to follow the call on her husbands life, even though it means placing herself in circumstances totally and terrifyingly foreign to her. There is hardship, deception and tragedy, all the elements of a good tale. Mostly, however, it is the story of two people, and their love for each other. It is the tale of devotion and love between a man and his wife, and the story of absolute love and trust in their God.

This is the telling of faith in the veracity of visions, given to men through the work of the Holy Spirit, in particular one vision. It is a tale of the devotion and dedication required to bring a vision once given and accepted into fruition, and the many miracles large and small which happened along the way.

We pick up our tale in late February 1982.

PART I

BEGINNINGS

FEBRUARY 1982

I awoke from a dark blackness, not the blackness of ordinary sleep, but that total nothingness induced by surgical anesthetics. To say that I awoke is not entirely true. It was more of an awareness, as my senses returned. An awareness that my eyes were open and that I existed.

At that moment my existence, the whole world if you will, was filled by a face. Only one face! A face covered with red, white and blue grease paint, topped by a frizzy red wig and an absurd hat. The face smiled, opened its mouth, and spoke, saying, "Jesus loves you Ken!" I smiled and drifted back into nothingness.

Six days earlier I had been kicked by a rather wild two year old stallion. I had suffered several broken ribs and as a result of the pain in breathing I had developed double pneumonia. My entire internal system had also shut down causing sever abdominal distention and a great deal of discomfort. All this had brought me to the hospital a day or two after the accident.

I had gone to the emergency room immediately following the event, that same day, which was a Saturday. This largely meant, while I was not ignored when I arrived at the hospital, the staff was only slightly interested in my injuries. I was given an x-ray, told I had a broken rib, given a handful of Tylenol 3 tablets and sent home with instructions to breath normally. Now how does one breath normally after being kicked with the full force of a 2000 lb horse? Completely ignored by these emergency room folks was the fact that the slightest breath almost caused me to black out.

When I arrived home I devoured the Tylenol 3 tables, did my best to follow orders, but as might be expected I rapidly got very sick and very miserable to say the least. Moreover, entirely missed by the folks in that hospital was something much, much worse than one broken rib.

On Monday morning I called my doctor, explained what had happened and how I was feeling. He immediately instructed me to meet him at the hospital, a different hospital, I lived 35 miles from where the incident had taken place.

I was so distended I could not bend over, almost passing out when I tried. I managed to slip my Levis on, but could not button them up and could not get my boots on at all. I managed to get into my pickup truck and drive the eight miles to the hospital, barefoot and undone. Once I arrived at the hospital, I faced the problem of extricating myself from the vehicle and walking the few yards to the emergency room. Somehow I managed, I was immediately admitted, and placed on the medical ward, because of the pneumonia and the accompanying fever.

My condition continued to deteriorate and by the end of visiting hours Thursday evening, I was thoroughly and completely miserable on two accounts. The one being more or less obvious by my physical condition, the second being brought on by my well meaning, but thoroughly misguided, friends from my church and Sunday school class. Over the course of the few days I had been so uncomfortably ensconced within the confines of the hospital, these good folks had managed to turn the torture I was already suffering into a sort of living hell of good old Christian guilt and crisis of faith.

I had accepted God's Grace of Salvation in Jesus some eighteen months earlier. Because I was alone on my little country homestead, I had immersed myself in the word, and I must say a lot of frantic prayer. I had grown rapidly, found a good church and several good mentors. I had a lot to learn at the time, yet I had even at this early and tender time, become a leader of sorts in the "mature" adult singles group at my church, and for the most part these good people were the cause of my secondary misery.

My friends, fueled by their own immaturity could not, or would not, accept that a "born again" child of God, "blessed with faith" so much as I, could be laying in a hospital virtually unable to move and steadily deteriorating. Hence the guilt!

Most of these good people had known the Lord a lot longer than I. They had heard a lot more messages by the great faith healers than I. Some had even been privileged to journey on pilgrimage to the dual fountains of faith, Oral Roberts University, and Reama Bible Collage in Tulsa. Some had even managed to bask personally under the direct tutelage of Oral Roberts and Kenneth Hagen Sr. themselves.

I realize the preceding statement sounds cynical, it is not meant to be, I merely wish to instill my feelings at the time. I have the greatest of respect for the work Oral Roberts and Kenneth Hagen Sr. later on in my walk with the Lord I benefited greatly from the teachings and lessons of both men. However, at the moment of the incidents being described here I was simply not mature enough, or schooled enough in my faith to deal with all the truth and error being heaped upon me by those who had managed to safely contain God in a box of their own making. This experience was one of the first "God boxes" I encountered. As I have grown and matured in my faith I have come to realize that God has a very disconcerting habit of ignoring the boxes we construct. It seems God is God after all and our confinements, so carefully constructed, just simply fail to contain our Omnipotent God, His attributes or desires for His creations.

As for me at that moment in time, that Thursday evening in February 1982, I knew without the doctors telling me, if they could not effect a turn around in my condition and quickly, I was dying. I was not delving into hysteria, this was just fact. There was something terribly wrong inside of me, and thus far it had not been discovered.

Oh Dear God! There must be something wrong with me! Have I completely missed you? My friends tell me that if I truly love you I would not, could not remain in this condition. I would accept the healing gained for me on that horrible cross, get up and walk out of here. Now!

Do I really love you? Is all that has happened to me since I met you and came to love you false? What terrible thing have I done? What have I missed? After all I am told by those who should know, that something like this does not happen to one who is walking pure and upright with God. I did not know it then, but I was to hear this last statement many times in the years to come. It is a statement I have come to regard as coming straight from the pit of hell itself.

This some what describes my condition and state of mind that Thursday evening as the nurse finally ran everyone out and the last prayers of faith and healing were pronounced over me. The sound of "by His stripes you are healed" faded from my ears and I was left in my misery and shame.

Alone I faced my God and Savior, broken, and hopeless, as I lay there, I was my own condemning tangible evidence that some how I had missed the mark. God, what a miserable wreck I was as I drifted of into a restless slumber, hoping against hope that God in His mercy would relent and accept me to His bosom as I died, even though I obviously was so unworthy.

Friday morning, 1:30am I awoke in the most incredible pain. Pain so intense I do not have words to describe. I managed to press the call button, and before anyone could answer I literally exploded from both ends. Gas, fluids, solids erupted from my body and I experienced momentary relief from the pain. Within seconds the pain returned, more demanding than ever, and short moments later nurses were scrambling about me attempting to determine just what had happened and to clean up the mess.

Unknown to everyone, the kick had ruptured my spleen, but not the tough membrane which surrounds this organ. My spleen had been filling with fluid all week. It had finally filled to bursting and exploded, shredding itself into a million pieces in the process. I was now bleeding to death internally and no one knew! The nurses cleaned me up shook their heads and went off to their other duties.

Some four hours later I recalled the nurse, telling her I was in terrible pain and that I could feel something was very, very wrong. She assured me it was only my imagination. However, she would tell her relief to notify the doctor when she came on duty at 7:00am.

By 6:30am I was in a really bad way. The pain was inconceivable, and the nurses by this time were also convinced something was very wrong. They were attempting to locate a doctor, any doctor, to come and determine what to do for me. The next hours are a blur, as far as time and chronology, yet not the events which transpired.

First was the pain. It was incredible. All consuming, white hot, searing until nothing remained of life or existence except pain. The pain just seemed to grow. I soon wanted nothing more than death. Death seemed to be the only possible manner of escape. Only Death could bring relief from something this powerful and all consuming. I began to pray out loud, begging for death. "please dear Jesus, please take me, please now! Take me home now, let me be with you. Take me home, stop the pain!

I remember it as if it all took place only moments ago. The two nurses working at my side became alarmed. I heard one of them on the phone, telling someone they had better hurry. I was in a kind of limbo, intensely aware of the pain, yet unable to focus my eyes. As I remember everything had taken on a sort of apricot glow. I was aware of people and activity around me, but could not really see clearly. Then it happened!

Suddenly, standing at the foot of my bed was a man. I could not tell who it was, but when He spoke, I knew instantly, without doubt, this man at the foot of my bed could only be the Lord Jesus himself!

I could not see His face, as it was in shadow from the glory light around Him, the soft golden apricot glow. There was no doubt who He was, there was no need to see His face or for introductions. He who was, He who is, He who is to come was standing at the foot of my bed. He just stood there saying nothing, not moving, just there!

"Oh! Thank you Lord you've come for me, come to take me home!" I said out loud. My two nurses, I was told later, panicked. They were both devoted Christian ladies, and although they could see no visitor in the room, both felt a presence with us in the room and neither could move around the foot of the bed.

As I gazed at my visitor standing at the foot of the bed He reached out, spreading His arms toward me and said, "No! You will be well for I have work for you to do." He stood silent for sometime, then He was gone. My pain left and I could see my surroundings clearly, as well as the startled, puzzled faces of my nurses. It was 10:30am.

Of all the bright nova like memories of this happening in my life, one stands out above all the others. The voice of the man standing before me at the foot of my hospital bed. When he spoke it was like being immersed in cool water. His voice was all there was, there was nothing else. His voice, his words, were totality. The substance of it filled every cell of everything, refreshing, providing sustenance and life. The effect was as being contained within a womb of perfection. At the moment of His speech nothing existed except that it existed within the sound of His voice. My words fail me and have failed me for years as I attempt to describe the voice. How does one describe the voice of the living God in mere mortal words. I shall never forget that voice, how could I? No wonder Saul was a changed man after hearing that voice on the road to Damascus. Although my words fail to be adequate, after hearing our Lord's voice I now understand John's beginning of his gospel, "in the beginning was the word and the word was with God". Our Lord Jesus is the very embodiment of the word, the very voice of God. What more proof need there be that He lives? God the Father is eternal. His voice never dies.

Jesus himself came to me as I lay in my misery in that hospital. He came to me! He told me I was to be well. So I was healed and got up from my bed and danced out of the hospital, right? WRONG!!

Although the pain was gone and I could see everything clearly, I was immobile. I could not move. All my vital signs indicated I was rapidly leaving this world. Finally the doctors and x-ray technicians agreed that something was wrong, though they knew not what it could be, and decided on exploratory surgery. This was around 11:00am, I was "rushed" into surgery at 1:30pm. I remember this event and time clearly, however by this time I could not open my eyes.

One of the doctors, there were two, was having trouble inserting a needle into a vein some where around my right shoulder. He was swearing a little, agitated because he could not get the IV started. "Don't worry, I said, but please hurry doctor I feel I don't have much time." I have no idea why I said this. Especially after all I had experienced just shortly prior to the present moments. He finally slipped the needle into place, turned on the drip and I passed into blackness.

I slowly became aware of my surroundings, I was elevated above everyone in the operating room, looking down upon the proceedings. I was at the head of the table looking at myself. I could see all the surgery staff frantically working over me. All of my intestines were outside my body, lying beside me and one of the people was busy cleaning the empty abdominal cavity. My abdominal cavity! The others were busy with other tasks, all were very bloody, blood was everywhere.

I was aware of myself suspended above this scene. I could not, however, see my legs or feet as I floated above the activity below. I knew I was dying. I could not hear any of the noise or the voices of the people working around my body. I just floated there watching, for how long I do not know, but it seemed a long while.

Suddenly the voice, the same voice I had heard earlier as the man stood at the foot of my bed, said, **"I said I have work for you to do!"**

Blackness, then bewilderment as I looked into the smiling red, white, and blue rodeo clown face of my friend Arthur telling me "Jesus loves you Ken."

∞◦❈◦∞

I learned some days later that while in surgery I had died for approximately ten minutes. Also while in recovery I had been given morphine for pain which had caused me to go into respiratory arrest. All of my blood was changed as quickly as possible. This occurred in full, living and graphic reality in front of two of my friends, my employer being one of them.

My friend Arthur's wife happened to be the chief duty nurse that afternoon and had called him at a rodeo in Altus Oklahoma, about 150 miles distant, telling him, "If you ever want to see Ken alive again, you had better come now!" He left immediately, without changing and came directly to my bedside. Today many years and miles distant, when I think on the events of that day in my life my memories always begin with the vision of my clown telling me "Jesus loves you Ken."

I awoke the morning after the surgery in my hospital room surrounded by people and filled with incredible pain. The physical pain was understandable, and almost as soon as my eyes opened the mental anguish brought on by the guilt, began anew as those well meaning souls around me began their healed and faith driven mantras. I was to be in the hospital until the last of May and had another surgery to correct the mistakes made by the first doctor. All the details of these months are not important. I remained in pain, all the while being injected with large amounts of high powered pain killer. However, I remained in pain, I simply did not get better. I weighed 120 lbs down from my normal 220 lbs. I was poked and prodded, given every test and scan know to medicine at the time, and I remained ill and in pain.

By this time the scar of the surgery had healed, leaving an angry red slash a half inch wide across my abdomen. My five broken ribs, not the one as I had originally been told, were as healed as ribs can ever be. Needless to say my doctors were stymied. Finally, I do not remember how, it was discovered the my gall bladder had ceased to function. It had not recovered from the trauma brought on by the shut down of my internal systems prior to the first surgery. Another surgery removed the defective organ, fixed a few other things found to still be undone from the other surgeries, and closed me up. Seven days later a drain device left in my abdomen as part of the gall bladder removal process was removed and I was pronounced cured. The next day I was discharged, sent home clutching a pillow to my abdomen, a physical and emotional wreck!

Several things happened during the three months I was trapped in that monument to pain and suffering they called a hospital.

After the first surgery I was surrounded by friends, mostly those from my Sunday school class, however, as time drug on they stopped coming. I must admit that except for one or two it was a real blessing when they stopped coming, for I was never free of their continuous recrimination. How can a true believer come to such a fate? Some of the more zealous became convinced it was their task to "get me saved." I truly was a test of their faith and maturity. I was told repeatedly, sometimes hourly, day after day, "You just need to quit feeling sorry for yourself. Get up out of that bed and go home. After all your supposed to be a born again believer, so how can you just lie there, your healed by His stripes, in Jesus name."

The most cruel of all, "Why Jesus himself came to this room, told you you were healed, (their words not His), so if that's true what are you still doing here?" I had told a few of my closest friends of the visitation and other experiences and of course it had spread quickly among my church group.

God, what a mess I was, how could I dispute what they said? How could anyone who had been visited personally by Jesus Himself still be in the condition I found myself? I was the most wretched of men choosing to remain in my flesh instead of picking up my pallet and walking away in victory. With this burden of despair and guilt heaped upon my head, I was ashamed to show my face. Gradually I came to believe what they were telling me and thankfully with one or two exceptions they stopped coming. I was to great a test of their faith, I was hopeless. I believe that the more honest of those, came to realize there must be some error in the things they were telling me and stopped coming out of their own embarrassment.

I wish to make it clear at this point, I believe in miraculous healing. In the years that have followed I have experienced a few myself, and have participated in a few through ministry. However, there is one crucial point I missed at the time, but discovered much later, a point those good brothers and sisters missed as well.

The Lord in His statement that day said I would be "well" not "healed." Seemingly a small difference, but a huge difference in the context of meaning. I was well, but, not healed in the natural. To this day, years later, the scars are still a painful reminder of the day Jesus visited me to make me aware of work I was to do. I was well, He was and is with me every step of the way, in the surgery, the months in the hospital, all the years since. I am not a linguist, but I know in my spirit, He chose His words carefully, for He is the Word. We must, I have learned, be very careful of our words, as Christ lives within us. The world does not know the difference between our words and His. When they look at us, they see, or are supposed to see, Jesus.

When we speak, they cannot tell whether we are speaking from our flesh or His. They cannot tell if we are allowing Him to speak through us at that moment. In truth they are not even aware of the difference, they are only aware of who we profess to be and if our words sound like theirs, they do not listen. They know who we are, we are stamped with His seal, to the world we are the enemy.

It is only our fellow Christians who rush through life, blindly filled with religious zeal and purpose, who do not recognize, let alone know their fellow warriors in Christ. I believe most of us are so busy convincing ourselves we are holy and righteous, that we forget to let Jesus live through us as He desires. As a result we walk by fellow believers, missing many of the blessings and miracles God preforms daily in our lives. We do this while continually crying out to the Lord for some "need" to be filled which we consider important at the time.

I am persuaded we as followers of the Lord Jesus must learn first to recognize each other, before we can recognize the enemy.

I am healed by His stripes, I was then and always will be and some day I will have no scares or pain.

However, most importantly "I am well in Christ Jesus".

FEBRUARY 1984

Sunday Morning. I am setting in a pew on the right side of the sanctuary in my church. It is a place I have not occupied for almost two years. Sunday school is not yet finished. Except for a few early birds sitting quietly with their thoughts, and their God, and the choir practicing, I am alone.

I too am talking quietly with my God. As I listen to Him, I am astonished as He reminds me that this day is two years to the day, since the day when He appeared to me in the hospital. The day my problems really began! I laughed out loud. Loud enough to attract a few frowns in my direction, "your not supposed to laugh in God's house you know." How ridiculous and sad we are in the concepts we have of our Father. More boxes I suppose.

It should be understood that my relationship with our Lord has always been very frank and straight forward. When I talk to Him I use the language and the brain He has given me. Believe it or not He generally talks back the same way. The primary difference being, He needs fewer words to get His point across. He does not talk to me in King James English, NIV, Revised Standard, or anything else we have conjured up to distance Him from us. He speaks to me in Oklahoma Cowboy with a slight Okie twang.

It has always puzzled me the way good believing folks turn into caricatures of themselves when they talk to the Lord. Standing rigid, white faced, speaking a foreign language, usually King James English, they cannot understand. How do we ever expect to know Him? The Scriptures tell us He meets us where we are, that He lives within us. I ask you, do we live in King James' England. Are we living at a time when only the nobility and the priests, and very few of them, were literate?

Largely the priests were the only ones who communicated in the high toned language of the King James bible. Even they spoke differently when they themselves were at home or away from court. Granted, they possessed a greater volume of vocabulary than we Americans do today, and doubtless used more fifty cent words, as my Grandfather used to say, in their conversations than can be found in our "modern" conversations. So how did we ever get the idea that conversations between ourselves and a God and Lord who dwells within us can only be held in a language which is as dead to us as the mackerel in the can on the pantry shelf?

Do not misunderstand me, I love the King James Bible. Its flowery prose makes one seem to be living the make believe of a grand Shakespearean actor of long ago, however, when I am seriously studying to learn of Him or to prepare to teach of Him I usually chose a different version. Our Lord and our life with Him is not make believe, grand or otherwise, it is real hard ball life. If you will be honest before Him, He will provide a life's worth of communication in language you will not have to struggle to understand. I believe His greatest joy is to talk with us. Does not Genesis tell us the very reason we were created is to be His companions? That means communication, talking with one another. I find no where within the scriptural record, instructions to learn King James, Quaker, Latin, Hebrew, Greek or church Speak, before He will speak with me or I can speak with Him. He Loves us, He died so He could talk to us. So why do we put Him behind this dark veil of "holy language"?

Talk to Him! He is our friend not our enemy!

When I came home from the hospital in late May 1982 my life was a shambles. Physically I was on the mend, I began to gain weight, my scars were sore and painful as they still are, but I was mending. However, emotionally I was a wreck.

Anyone who has ever suffered a major trauma and spent several months in the hospital knows where I was emotionally. My greatest desire was to get out of that place and return to my life, friends, and church. I found instead that I had lost all confidence in myself and my abilities. I found myself in a kind of limbo, unsure of my ability to preform even the simplest task. Tasks which before I had accomplished without even a conscious thought, now required enormous effort. I had an irrational fear of the scars opening unexpectedly and finding my insides in the bed or floor next to me. Needless to say this state was not understood or accepted by those around me.

I was an Architect, the ranch, its stock and all things associated with it were my avocation. I found as I returned to work I could not make my hands and mind move the pencil and equipment to create the details and drawings which had been second nature prior to the accident. I could not concentrate, my mind was always somewhere else. Physically I could not sit at the drafting board more than a few minutes, but the greatest problem was my lack of concentration and confidence. As you can imagine this did not sit well with my employer and by September of that year I found myself unemployed with no prospects.

The one bright spot during this time was a lady I have come to cherish as my sister. Judy was employed as a real estate consultant by the same Architecture firm as myself. She had visited me at the hospital a time or two, as I remember she and her husband Lowrie, were the only ones I was glad to see and did not want to leave. We had also shared our faith briefly a time or two prior to the accident. After my return to the world outside the hospital she seemed to be the only one who grasped even a small portion of my state of being. We had many long conversations and prayers, to the detriment of her income, I suspect. We grew to know and love each other greatly as brother and sister. Judy's husband Lowrie, who is a United Methodist Pastor and Elder, has also become a great friend and brother. I have considered him to be my pastor for all these years, even when we have been separated by time and distance. More than any one person Judy is responsible for bringing me back from the brink.

My friends and church did not understand or accept me. Spiritually I was as big a mess as I was emotionally. Most of those who bothered to concern themselves with my condition saw no deeper than the surface, where physically I was improving rapidly. I had been convinced while in the hospital that at the very least I was an ingrate for allowing my condition to deteriorate and not walk in health despite my injuries, as I was supposed to do.

The first Sunday morning out of the hospital, I sat on a folding chair in my Sunday school class, holding my pillow to my scars to take the pressure, so I could sit upright. My 120lbs of skin and bones made the others present in the class uncomfortable and I seemed to be a rebuke to them. I was very quickly made to be unwelcome and unloved.

How dare I, a child of God, if indeed I were, appear in this condition. Was I not specially set apart? Had I not received a special commission, much the same as Saul had been given some 2000 years before on the road to Damascus? How could I appear among them a physical, emotional and spiritual fraud! They seemed to forget that Saul was blind for a season and carried "a thorn in the flesh" for the remainder of his life as the price of his commission.

God forgive them, for they had no mercy. By the end of June I could no longer face them, my church, or even my God. The army of God had almost succeeded in killing its wounded. I ran for what was left of my life. I no longer had the safety of the communion of the church which had been so important to me. I believed at this point that I was a fraud as a "Christian" so I decided to hide myself from God. Yet, even at this I was a miserable failure. God found me everywhere I went. For eighteen months I tried to hide, I refused to accept His call. I said things to Him I do not want to repeat, yet, He was always there reminding me, **"I have work for you to do."**

Four people in all the world had not given up on me and declared me lost. Judy and Lowrie, and Ed and Ruth. Ruth although younger than me, seemed like a mother to me and big Ed, with his knowing smile would just reach out a large friendly hand, grasp my shoulder in an iron grip, and keep me firmly planted in this life.

Ruth was always telling me, "Ken your called to ministry. God has a very special work for you. Why don't you just accept it and end the turmoil in your life? You know you'll never have any peace until you do!" I would always mumble something and leave as quickly as possible.

I will always remember Christmas 1982. I spent that Christmas with Ed, Ruth and their children. That evening after the children were in bed we adults were enjoying the fire, friendship and the season, when Ruth did it again. "Ken when are you going to come to your senses, come back to the Lord and take up the ministry you have been given? Ed and I can't stand to see you like this. Jesus loves you so much, why can't you accept your call?

I hung my head and said, "Ruth I am only going to say this once. Since I was in the hospital and ever since, day and night, without ceasing, the Lord has bombarded me with this call, this ministry thing, to the point I'm about to go nuts. You know the hell I've been through, but I know myself, I know who I am. How in the world am I ever going to accomplish a cock-o-mamie scheme like He wants me to do? It's got to be the dumbest thing I've ever heard in my life. I can't even get well from a stupid accident. How in God's name am I supposed to do this ministry thing?"

"I know from where I come, I'd be laughed out of town if I declared myself in ministry. To top that I don't what to be a preacher! Lord! The very thought makes me want to hide in a hole! I don't care what He does to me, He knows I love Him, but He can beat me to a bloody pulp and I'm still not going to be a Preacher. For that matter I'm not going to get involved in the stupid plan He keeps playing over and over in my head and before my eyes. I just can't do it. He can get someone else! Someone like Copeland, or Roberts, you and Ed. If you guys believe in this so much why don't you do it?"

Why they are still my friends I do not know. I guess they realized I was pouring out months of frustration, that, and Ruth's stubborn faith in God and His call on my life.

"Ken you don't mean that", Ruth said.

"Oh but I do, I love Jesus, and I know I am going to be with Him some day. But if He takes what little I've got left, beats me into a fat pile of blood and guts I am not going to be a preacher and that's that!

Little did I know!

I did not see Ed and Ruth for the next fourteen months. I saw Judy only once during that time, a chance meeting in a restaurant. I managed to completely disappear from my friends lives. I could not, though I tried, disappear from God.

During the next months I was to see my career as an Architect dissolve before my eyes, to the point I could not secure any form of work remotely related to Architecture. As a matter of fact I could not secure any kind of work, period. My ranch and the stock all went to pay the doctor and hospital bills. Every worldly possession I owned disappeared. Eventually even my clothing.

By September 1983 I was stripped bare. I found myself living in a friends home while they were overseas. The Lord, even then was faithful to see that I had shelter and food, but I had nothing else. I saw nor spoke to no one from early September 1983 to early January 1984, except for brief trips once a week(unemployment checks) to the grocery store. Two days a month my nine year old daughter Amanda would stay with me. I lived for those visits, and tried to hide the truth about my situation from her. I do not think I was successful even in that. Those months were not much fun for her I am afraid. She loved her daddy and her visits kept me going.

All this time I kept a running dialog with the Lord. I kept asking how to change my situation. Asking for His help, pleading with Him at times for mercy. Always I would get the same answer. That wonderful voice would say, **"Do that which I have asked of you."**

I continued to refuse, "Lord I don't want to be a dammed Preacher. Just let me love you, just let me be happy with you, please."

"Do that thing which I have asked of you." always the reply.

I did not relent and neither did He. I just became poorer. More and more isolated and each day more like the fat pile of bloody pulp I had so vividly described on that Christmas eve some months before. I was given no rest during this time. Constantly day in day out, twenty four hours a day, awake or asleep, before my eyes and mind, in glorious color, was played out detail upon detail the work I was to do. This process never ended. I begged for release, but my requests fell upon deaf ears. Always, **"Do that thing which I have asked of you."** Always until I was completely broken and stripped. A fat pile of bloody pulp, almost convinced I was insane. Yet unbelievably I continued to say no.

In January even the provision of food and shelter were stripped away. I found myself on the streets in the middle of one of the coldest January's Oklahoma had seen in many years. Two weeks prior I had finally taken a door to door sales job, the only thing I could find. I was befriended by a fellow worker and taken into his home. All though he did not know the Lord, and most defiantly not living for Him, he and his wife took pity on me. Over the next several weeks they helped me get established and the Lord blessed them and me for a season.

By this time I had reached the point of submission. However, I still had not said yes to the Lord. To tell the truth at this stage I believe my recalcitrance was anchored more in the over all impossibility of it all, rather than any rebellion against God. Never-the-less, I was certainly tired of being beaten up! More importantly because of the constant "mind video", a process which has not stopped, I was becoming more and more convinced, in my spirit, that this whole ridiculous scheme just might be possible, and that I just might be able to carry it off, but I had not yet said yes.

February 19, 1984. I found myself sitting in my old church, in my old position, on my old pew being reminded by the Lord of February 19, 1982 and His provision for me. I broke. I found myself saying to Him, "Yes Lord I will do the thing which you have asked of me. I think your crazy, but I love you. I will do it."

I felt a hand on my shoulder. I turned to look into the big smile of my friend big Ed. "It's about time," he said.

BUILD MY BOAT AND PREACH MY WORD THE VISION

"Do that thing which I have asked of you."** This is what the Lord told me over and over. I will explain the vision and list it in some detail.

The process began while I was in the hospital in 1982 and has continued to this day. There have been days of rest and periods so intense all I could do was sit and let it be presented. However, I do not remember a day since early 1982, in which some portion of this ministry vision has not been portrayed before me.

There are several steps or parts to this plan. The first is told here, others will follow, as they were reveled to me in the sequence of this story.

The vision is played out to me through my minds eye, and at times in front of my eyes, something like a motion picture screen only with me in the middle of the action. The process comes and goes, lasts for hours or days at a time. The process once lasted for nine months without a break, 24 hours per day. I was able to function normally, whatever is considered normal for someone in my situation. I could work and so forth, but the pictures were always there occupying half my brain and senses, awake or asleep.

The process is captioned with dialog only sparsely, such as, "do this________". Then the pictures start in full color and three dimensional detail. Details even to slight imperfections in paint finishes. I have come to realize over the years, these things the Lord is showing me already exist. They have already been done in His world, and in ours, somewhere in the future. He is simply giving me the tour, so I will know how these things are to be accomplished.

This is not fatalism on my part. I can still choose to say no. I can choose the wrong direction or even the wrong people, if I do not pay close attention. I have done this in the past a few times and most likely will do it again. I am only human and for some reason there were a great many details He left out of His very detailed instructions. These, for the most part, are the items which require me and others, but especially me to walk in faith. Faith which requires complete dependence upon Him to provide the means with which to take the next step.

I have found this "faith walk" something most of us find very easy to write about, talk, about, even tell others how to do, very difficult to maintain. We even have the ability to convince ourselves as we go about our daily lives under our own steam, that some how we are living by faith. I am hear to tell you after many decades of experience in working through this vision and other aspects of life, that it takes and extreme amount of focus on the Lord to get it right.

Frankly for the most part, we fail miserably. For instance, when faced with an impossible circumstance where only the provenience of God can provide the solution for the need, how do we choose? I have discovered that inevitably, if we "tarry", some person or thing will present it's self as the solution. How do we know if the solution is from the Lord or from some other source? If we choose the presented solution are we acting in faith or are we merely accepting someones solution to the problem and in the process relinquishing part of the vision into their control?

It takes a well focused and discerning mind and spirit to tell the difference. Most of the time we fool ourselves by convincing ourselves we are walking in faith, with the Lord firmly in control, when in fact we ourselves are firmly in control. Others will always attach themselves to another persons vision and offer solutions. It is the responsibility of the person who "owns" the vision to discern if the solutions being offered fall in line and conform to the details presented, if not then they must be rejected. I must confess I was not too awfully good at this process in the beginning and made many decisions which came back to haunt me later as our story will reveal.

There are three forces active in this world, the Lord, Satan, and people or ourselves. The first two are talked about all the time, the third hardly ever. The first two go unseen, the third is constantly before us, and is usually responsible but rarely held to account.

To make life even more complicated we are constantly being bombarded with fact, and a lot of fiction, about the reality of the other two. It is little wonder the third member of this particular trinity, ourselves, takes over so easily allowing us to convince ourselves just as easily that we are the source and control of all things.

We all know the stories of great faith. Our problem comes in not being able to apply the principles taught in them to our own situations. A man I know once told me this story. This man is very successful in his chosen career and openly declares he owes it all to the Lord. He is totally committed to living his life by faith in every aspect. He was preparing to leave for the office one morning. He paused in front of his dressing room mirror. He stood admiring himself in a particularly flattering new sports jacket. "Lord your so good to me," he said, "thank you for this new jacket you have given me."

"I did not give you the jacket," came the answer, loud and clear. **"You gave yourself the gift."**

My friend was immediately struck with realization that his faith was mostly in himself and his abilities, not in God's. True, because he believed, he was blessed "coming in and going out." However, he concluded that because his confidence in his own abilities was so strong, his faith rested mostly in himself. As a result he had missed many of the things God had wanted to give to him. Can you imagine the jacket God had in mind?

Hind sight is wonderful. I know now that my refusal to accept the challenge the Lord had presented to me had little to do with my not wanting to be a preacher, but everything to do with faith. I had no faith in my own abilities to accomplish the goals set for me in the vision. I knew that if all I had was myself, I was doomed to failure. I am ashamed to admit I had not put my trust in the Lord to do the work. I had forgot, or maybe I did not yet know, I only needed to let Him do it through my faith in His divine wisdom and abilities.

It took eighteen months to rebuild in me what had been destroyed by my fellow Christians and myself. I had to believe in Christ within me once more. I knew that in myself I could not even begin to accomplish the tasks set before me in the vision. I had to relearn faith. Once learned it is not automatic., it must be refreshed daily, sometimes more frequently. One of the "tricks" is to learn to recognize the signs of His presence with us. Even though He is unseen, as He walks with us, it is possible to see the physicality of His presence in the things He does around us as we make our way through this life.

Learn to know His hand and little by little it will become more clear and somewhat easier, but, ah the caveat, the challenge is always to discern His hand from the hand of others, as we move through our lives and mission.

I personally have seen many wondrous things since I began my walk with the Lord, August 19, 1980. A few of them will be recounted in this telling. I have walked on the edge, with only faith in my Lord for the next step of my foot. Yet, I am constantly fighting myself to remember it is He who is in control, not I. Some days and times I am more successful than others.

⸺∘∘∘❈∘∘∘⸺

The visions appeared quite simply, I heard the voice say, **"I will send you to the islands of the sea to be a new song for My Son. Build My boat and preach My word, preach My word and build My boat."**

All the while I was suspended above the earth, more exactly over the oceans. I could see hundreds of ships sailing from port to port. Some were sailing vessels, some were power vessels. All bore the same markings, colors, and flags. All of them flew as owners pennants, the Christian flag.

This particular scene with its message was played over and over many times, during the next weeks and months. So many times, in fact, I lost count. It is occasionally repeated to this day. Perhaps when

23

I need reminding of the overall commitment I have made. Next began the most intensive portion to date, or perhaps I have grown accustomed to the intensity as time passes.

I was placed upon the deck of a sailing vessel. She was under full sail. Her sails were set to catch the strong breeze coming over her starboard rail, just forward of midships.

I could feel the breeze on my face and in my hair. The roll and pitch of her decks as she worked through the seas was very real and exciting. I could see, as well as hear, the bow wave as it rolled down her side. The sights and sounds of a sailing ship, under full sail, in open sea, were everywhere. I was alone upon her decks. I was immediately in love.

At this point I was taken off her deck to a point which seemed to be about eighty feet distant or so on her starboard side. I could see her clearly as she moved through the water. She was painted white with blue trim, rub rails and chain boards. Her rig was that of a bald headed schooner. She had two masts and a single bowsprit without a striker. She was gaff rigged with full main, foresail, fore stay sail and jib set. Upon the leech of the main, approximately three fourths of the distance to the gaff, was set the Stars and Stripes. On the main mast starboard signal hoist flew the Christian flag.

I could see she had hard chines, with a moderate "V" bottom. At least the portion of her hull exposed due to her heel indicated this to be the case. Her shear and bows were very full, making for dry decks and plenty of flotation, keeping her from plowing through the waves as she plunged into the troughs between the seas. She had turned spindles supporting the rails along her decks. Her deck was divided into four sections. The first was a small anchor deck at the bow where the bow spirit was attached. Second, raised about a foot above the first was the main deck, large and flat from just forward of the foremast aft to the mainmast. Third, the quarter deck raised at the mainmast and continued aft to a point over the keel known as the horn. Fourth and finally a Poop deck aft from the quarter deck, out over the horn to the stern rail. As she sailed by, across her stern I could see two rather large stern ports to light her after cabin. Down her side were five smaller ports for the interior spaces. The white and blue colors continued across her stern in the appropriate areas. Her bottom was black, with the copper green hue which comes from the anti-fouling ingredients contained in modern bottom paint. As she sailed by, a lovelier sight would be hard to imagine. Across her stern, above the stern ports, emblazoned in dark blue letters was her name and hailing port.

MARANATHA

Okla. City, Okla.

This particular portion of the vision was repeated three times, by itself, in three days time. It then was repeated each time the next part was started. After seeing her sail by I would be taken to shore, to a work place something like a boat yard.

The same vessel would be standing there in stocks. I could see her entire hull, keel, rudder, and standing rig. Invisible hands would begin to dismantle her piece by piece, detail by detail. Although I was not doing the work myself, I was some how right in the middle of every detail. I saw every timber, plank, nut, bolt, nail and screw.

When the dismantling was completed, reassembly began, every piece from the beginning to completed vessel. This process was repeated twenty four hours a day for months. It always started or more accurately restarted, with me standing on her deck as she sailed through the sea. Always ending as the mast head truck was installed on the mainmast. Always restarting immediately, like a continuous loop.

No dimensions were ever given. She was constructed of plywood with wood ribs and keel. She was full keeled with a large half heart shaped rudder inboard under the horn. She carried accommodations for a crew and a cargo hold amidships. She was built in a rather traditional fashion except for the use of plywood and epoxy glues.

I would ask the Lord what this was all about, my answer was always the same, **"Build My boat and preach My word, preach My word and build my boat."**

This was the ministry vision I was struggling with that Christmas night when I unloaded upon poor Ruth, an all those months right up until the time I submitted and told the Lord I would do it, February 19,1984.

There then started a period of rest. The visions while not stopping reduced in frequency and intensity. I seemed to be left to my own devices or vices as the case might be, however, for a period of months all appeared to be relatively normal in my life.

Some months later the visions began with intensity and urgency once again. I was soon to learn this was because the Lord had finally managed to convince a certain young lady to give up her "security blanket" in Nebraska and move to Oklahoma. A young lady who became a central character to this tale.

1984 AND RUBBER SOUP

1984 was a very eventful year.

Toward the end of January, my friend and I decided to start a business. It was a small special coatings business, dealing in epoxy paints, coatings and waterproofing systems mainly. We also had a third but mostly silent partner. We had very little capital, I had none. Nevertheless we prospered, though we were always struggling to meet payroll. By midsummer we were doing pretty well and by the end of the year we had completed approximately $100,000.00 in contracts. Not a great deal but excellent considering we started with just $500.00 cash and a whole lot of raw nerve.

I believe the reasons we prospered are two fold. First the Lord need me to learn about epoxy resins and establish sources of supply. Connections which became crucial as time passed. Secondly and more importantly I insisted that as a corporation we tithe. As payments were received on our various projects, prior to anything else being paid or purchased, the tithe, ten percent of the gross, was deducted. Since the three of us, the partners, all professed connections to different churches, we divided the tithe equally among us, sending or taking our portion to the church of our choice. The funds were to be given in the name of the company not in the name of the individual partner. At least this is the way it worked for myself and my friend. Our silent partner insisted that his portion be given to him, as he wished to deliver his portion personally.

As I have said before you cannot fool God!, Eventually I was to discover he was not using the funds as agreed but was simply depositing the checks into his own account. Acquiring this knowledge was to assist in my departure from the company at a later date. However for the present we prospered.

By the end of the year we had grown from just the three original partners into and organization of ourselves, with ten employees and several thousand dollars in contracts and equipment.

We had little in the bank, but somehow the funds always seemed to be there when we needed them. The Lord blessed our tithe even though a portion was being withheld from Him. I wonder sometimes what would have happened if all the tithe had been freely given. My friend did not understand, but as long as he could see the increase he was a willing tither. He and his wife even started attending church occasionally.

All this time in the back of my mind was the promise I had made the Lord to follow His instruction, **"build My boat and preach My word, preach My word and build My boat."** I looked upon the business as the means by which the necessary funds would be provided to build the vessel and fund the mission. I had not been shown this or given a time table, but it seemed reasonable to me.

Remember what I have said about helping God and being in control? What I had done. as I was to discover, was to build as nice box around this whole thing placing myself in control of how what when and where. I have come to believe that our Lord's prayer on the cross, "forgive them for they know not what they do." was not just for our having placed Him there on that particular day, but for all the times we place Him second to our own decisions for our lives. I have come to believe it was for our complete human condition. Separate as we are in this world, separated from God, for in all that we do, "we know not what we do." I believe we should conclude our prayers at all times with, "Lord your will be done on earth as in heaven, and please Lord forgive us for we know not what we do!"

I had started attending my church once again. I had not, however rejoined the adult singles group. I simply did not wish to be part of that involvement once more. The singles group had changed in the years that had passed. The members were new to me, most of them, and they appeared to be more interested in male female bonding than the things of the Lord. I had been single for several years now and the last thing I wanted was involvement with a woman, any woman, especially with all I had going on now. With the business and the vision I had all on my plate I needed or wanted.

I was quite content to remain single. I had experienced all the marriage I wanted, and believe me when it came to the subject of marriage, I did not know what I was doing! I was happy in my single state. The Lord and I had communion each morning, with study and prayer. Best of all there was no one to interfere or criticize. I could say what I thought without anyone casting a raised eyebrow in my direction. I spent my leisure time on the lake sailing with friends. My business was growing and for the first time in two plus years, my life was peaceful.

I know I am painting a rather idyllic picture. There were problems, but compared to what had passed just recently, life was a piece of cake. During this time I grew stronger physically and spiritually. My daily communion times with the Lord were wonderful. I was taught so much about covenant and His promises to us. He and I talked for hours. First I grew to know Him and love Him as my friend, then my brother, and finally as my Lord and King. During this time I allowed all He has for us to become part of my life and become the active ingredient of my day to day existence. I was having a blast!

Then came a fateful day in June.

Some years before as a tradition after Sunday evening service, I had started going to the Western Sizzler in the same town as my church. It was located close by the church so it was convenient for an after church snack before I began my twenty mile drive home. My favorite was the Soup and Salad Bar. I always had rubber soup. This consisted of whatever soup struck my fancy, usually French onion, or some form of chowder. I would top this steaming bowl of tasty delight with enough grated Mozzarella cheese to turn it into a creation closely resembling melted rubber. I began to invite others to join me and soon Sunday evenings, at the "Sizzler" became and extension of the adult Sunday school group as we gathered to partake of fellowship and rubber soup. When I returned to the church I discovered this still to be the tradition. No one currently involved knew I was the one who had started this weekly gathering. I had not been back very long when I was approached to join the group at the "Sizzler" after church. I accepted and joined them. I enjoyed the rubber soup, but otherwise I was very disappointed, it was just not the same. I do not know why I was surprised, nothing ever stays the same. The only constant in the universe is constant change.

The conversations seemed to be directed more toward scoring in the bedroom than anything else. It is not that the old group were saints by any stretch, but we did seem to direct the majority of our time and conversations toward overcoming our weakness and carnality, rather than simply, abjectly, and openly, giving in to that side of our lives, in an attempt to find a new lover. I finished my soup and excused myself. I did not rejoin the Rubber Soup set for a few weeks.

I believe that my reaction to the Rubber Soup crowd was partially due to my anti-female state at the time. I was very much satisfied with being single and had no room for female complications in my life. My daughter Amanda and our father-daughter relationship was all the feminine contact I needed.

The Lord and I were doing just fine by ourselves, thank you!

One particularly "springlike" evening in June, I decided to go to evening church. I had driven from the south side of Oklahoma City where I lived at the moment and had a nice time at church. I was working my way out of the building when I met an old acquaintance. Charles and I had not seen each other since my accident, so we decided to go to the "Sizzler" to visit. We discovered upon arriving that the only seating available was in a large booth with some of the singles group. We got our soup and sat down next to two ladies.

One of the ladies had been present during the time previous and recognized me. She immediately struck up a conversation, be it ever so one sided on her part, for I was there to visit with Charles not her. The other one said very little, she sat between myself and the chatty one and seemed a little embarrassed at the attempts of the woman on her other side to capture my attention. Since we were sitting rather close I could not help but notice a few things about her.

She had rather long, well groomed fingernails, she was nicely dressed in the way some women have of coordinating everything. She had short hair. Cut very close, a little rebellious, but also stylish for the time. She also wore the reddest lipstick I had ever seen. She was most definitely not a country girl, this one had big city written all over her.

The lady on her other side, her name was "Letta", was busily trying to attract my attention for more than casual conversation. Not that I was such a great catch, but I suppose I was sort of a mystery man at the time, and to this poor woman, any man was the right man at that noteworthy point in her life. Charles and I exchanged knowing smiles, he being a bachelor of long standing, and generally was left alone by the ladies in the adult singles, as unattainable.

I decided the one setting next to me was safe as far as I was concerned. She definitely did not fit into any lifestyle I had ever lived or could foresee for myself. I decided the only way I could get "Letta" off my back was to leave, something I was not yet ready to do, or strike up a conversation with this other woman.

"So what do you do?" I asked kind of hoarsely. God, what a dumb way to start a conversation.

"I work at the Velvet Dove." She said, as disinterested as I in really having a conversation. We exchanged a few meaningless pleasantries, I finished my soup, made my excuses and departed. I had gotten "Letta" off my trail and the other one, "Debbie" her name was, would not bother me. She definitely was not my type nor I hers. I was safe. I had escaped safely from the grasp of feminine clutches and would see neither of them again.

How wrong could a guy be!

THE BOYS

The writing of this tale finally began as the result of a visit with my now adopted sister Judy, and her husband Lowrie in their home. This was the first time we had seen each other in three years or so, and it was during our conversations that Judy convinced me the story was worth the writing.

As I began, I believed it to be only the story of the S/V Maranatha. Not being a writer, I turned to the Lord asking for His help in telling the story. I had tried at various times over the years to put some of the events down on paper without success. This time seems to be right however, and the words seem to glide from my pen. He has directed my hand and mind as to the writing, yet thus far, there has been little about the S/V Maranatha.

I had intended at this point to tell of my wife Debbie, yet as I gathered my thoughts to tell of her, I was impressed that I must tell you something of myself first. This is a task I do not relish, nevertheless, the Lord will not let me proceed until I do this particular thing.

I was born in Twin Falls, Idaho, July 24, 1940. I am the first born of Kenneth Alvin Linnell and Inola Gentry Linnell, My mothers family had moved to Idaho to escape the Oklahoma dust bowl. My father and his brother Eldred, "Uncle Bo", came to Idaho as recruits in the Civilian Construction Corp.

My parents met and fell in love while picking "spuds" in one of Idahos famous potato fields. They married, over the protestations of her family and ten months later, nature being what it is, here I am.

I am told that other than my mother, who he adored, my father's one great passion was to tell whomever he met of the love of Jesus. My aunt Bernice, one of mothers older sisters, told me all he ever wanted to talk about was the Lord, my mother, and his children. I have very few memories of him, but those I do have bear witness to the fact he was a very happy man. A man who loved life and who was loved deeply by those around him.

Shortly after my birth my parents returned to my fathers home town of Goodland, Kansas. Here my father entered the ministry as part time pastor of a small Methodist church in the north western corner of Kansas.

To feed his family, pay the bills, and save enough money to attend seminary, he went to work on the Rock Island railroad as a fireman. He was thus employed at the out break of World War II. His job was considered essential to the war effort and he was refused entry into the armed services. He and his brother, "BO", had been inseparable all of their lives, and yet only "Bo" went off to war. I have been told the saddest day of my fathers life was when his brother left for boot camp without him in December 1941.

My father was to never see his brother again. My father was killed in the early morning hours of January,19,1945. While his east bound freight sat on a siding near Flagler, Colorado, a west bound fast freight loaded with war materials, flew through a faulty switch onto the siding where my fathers train waited. My father was the only fatality of the resulting collision.

My mother never recovered. My memories of her prior to my fathers death are of a happy, smiling woman, warm and tender. After that time I do not remember seeing her smile. At the time of my fathers death they had three children, myself, my sister Clara Voncil, who died at eighteen months of age, and my brother, Bobby Dale. My mother was pregnant with a fourth child who was born February,14,1945, just short of one month later.

Shortly after Bill was born, she left my brothers and I with our fathers family and disappeared from our lives. She would reappear off and on for the next five years at various intervals to make attempts at making a home for us, never quite succeeding. During this time she remarried several times none of which lasted more than a few months or days in some cases. During this period she was in a sever auto accident, none of us knew where or when. This left her with a very pronounced limp and other injuries which ultimately were contributing factors in her death.

I have never found fault with my mother for her abandonment of her children to the care of their "Uncle Bo" and his family. Some how I understood her love for my father was so deep, and the wounds of his death so great, that she spent the last five years of her life attempting to replace the one great love of her life.

During the summer of 1949 she reappeared. It is one of the comforts of my memories of her, because at last she had found some measure of peace. She was married and living in California. We had a baby brother named Dennis and she was pregnant with who was to be our sister Sherrie.

"The boys" as we were called, happily returned with her to California, our noses glued to the windows of the train car all the way from Goodland to Las Angeles. One of the great adventures of our lives.

My mother died of a brain aneurism, brought on by complications remaining from her injuries received in that long ago auto accident, while giving birth to my sister Sherrie. It was January 19, 1945, five years to the day of my fathers death.

"The Boys" were not allowed to attend the funeral and four days later "Uncle Bo" arrived from Kansas. "The Boys" were loaded bag and baggage into "Uncle Bo's" Plymouth and we made the long drive back to Kansas. There was not much sadness or many tears from us, for this was just one more time away from our mother to be added to the list. We did not really understand that our mother was dead and that now we were truly orphans. It was just one more separation, much the same as before, since our fathers death. There had never been a bond with our step father, simply not enough time had elapsed. "The Boys" were to spend several years before the realization our mother was never ever going to come for us again finally became reality.

Our Uncle Bo was not married at this time. He had returned from Europe with a mild form of battle fatigue, what we now refer to as PTSD. He had gone ashore as a member of the army engineer corp on "D Day" and as he told me years later, he had walked all the way to Berlin. All the way there he had worked clearing mines, building bridges and such, while seeing his buddies and companions die all around him. He never received a scratch, he spoke of this time to me only once and that after I had married and had children of my own. But, he drank.

Shortly after our return from California our grandfather died. Uncle Bo decided that Grandmother Linnell, his step mother, had enough to do caring for her children still at home, without adding us, her step grandchildren, to the mix. Since he was in no shape to provide a home for himself, let alone us, he decided we should live with our mothers parents in Idaho.

Once more "The Boys" were loaded up into the Plymouth and made the long journey west to Idaho. This time we were traveling to the home of our mothers parents, people who we had never met. People who we had heard the grownups speaking of only guardedly, as one speaks of strange things hidden in the dark. For "The Boys" this was to be a dark and gloomy trip filled with dread at it's end. This epic journey transpired prior to my tenth birthday in the spring of 1950.

My mothers people were a totally different world than any we had know before. They owned a small vegetable farm on the eastern edge of Nampa, Idaho. They were hard working people who had lived hard lives. They had survived life as share croppers in Oklahoma, survived the dust bowl and the great depression by the hard work of their bent backs and calloused hands. They were not affectionate people and to "The Boys" they were old very, very old. My mothers youngest sister was only sixteen at the time, so I suppose they were not much older than fifty something, but to us they were old and very set in their ways.

Consequently for three young orphan boys, though we did not know it then, who desperately needed love and affection, along with time to heal, this was not the right place to find ourselves.

Years later I discovered that my mothers parents had never forgiven her for marrying my father, he was Methodist and they were Church of Christ, a state akin to being the spawn of Hades in their minds. They had rejected her when she had turned to them for support after my fathers death and were deeply angered when she had had Uncle Bo appointed as our guardian. This was the atmosphere "The Boys" were surrounded with for the next seven years.

We lived daily being told how evil our "Uncle Bo" and the rest of our fathers family were, until eventually we accepted it as the truth. Bill, at the time just five years old, was doted over and soon learned how to manipulate his way in or out of anything. Bob, eight years old, and I, ten almost, were put to work in the fields, literally from sunup to sundown. During those days the greatest two days of the year were the day school started and the day we returned to school after Christmas break. The worst was the last day of school for the year.

I have no fond memories of my mothers parents, so I must be careful how I treat them here. I believe they were honest people who believed they were right in what they did. However, for three boys such as us, it was not the right place. If ever an analysis of "The Boys" and the roots of their problems in coping with this life were to be made, this period of our lives would surely be found to be largely responsible. We came out of this place three thoroughly screwed up individuals.

When asked some years later why he had taken us to my mothers parents, more importantly why he had left us there, "Uncle Bo" told me that at the time there was no other choice. He also believed, given his knowledge of the family, that we would be better off if he remained out of the picture. "Too many cooks spoil the broth," he said. However, he was not to know the conditions under which we existed. When he did find out, seven years later, he immediately removed us from their care.

However, for my two brothers it was too late, for they forever afterward had great difficulty adjusting to life in a normal world, if such exists. I had ran away, lied about my age, forged signatures on enlistment papers, and joined the military. I was caught after a few months and discharged. When I was sent back to Nampa by the military I found refuge with a family in town. This ultimately became the reason "Uncle Bo" found out what was going on with us. After my seventeenth birthday I joined the US Air Force September 3, 1957.

DETRITUS
OR
FALLOUT OF A MISSPENT YOUTH

My brothers and I grew up not knowing how to love or be a family. We simply never had an example to follow. We obviously did not know the Lord, even after being dragged to every church service held at the Church of Christ in Nampa.

What we did see made us want to be just the opposite. However, we have spent our lives looking for love and acceptance. People always seem shocked when they learn of my family history, thinking the events of our lives would have brought "The Boys" very close to one another, just the opposite occurred. God knows we tried!

The first thing I did upon reaching twenty one was to take the guardianship away from "Uncle Bo." This is an act I am not proud of now, but, at the time I was still filled with years of mistrust and I believed it to be the correct action. No matter what action my brothers and I took to be a family, all failed. At the time of this writing I have not seen my brother Bob in many years, and it has been three or four since we have spoken by telephone. Brother Bill was ever the enigma, enlisting in the Navy upon graduating high school, he appeared just five weeks later with a medical discharge. He had finagled the Navy into this, by marching off the end of a peer, or so he said. Bill was never much to be believed. Over the next several years he would just appear as though from nowhere and disappear just as quickly. I never knew where he was between these times of appearing and disappearing. I am sad to say Bill passed away some fifteen years ago, an event I only learned of years after his passing. He was married, apparently happily, and had a large brood of children, I do not know how many. His wife and all his family are convinced to this day that I am the incarnation of Satan himself, so I never hear from or much of them.

The circumstances of my growing up years affected my life with a very deep seated rebellious nature, mistrust of others, and a constant search for love and approval. Strange, since as I know now, that when I found it I could not recognize it. Up to the point where I met face to face with the Lord, I was very proud to say I had done it all myself. I had clawed my way up to the top, gotten an education, and was considered a success in my chosen career. I had money, cars, planes, boats and I had done it all myself. I had clawed my way to the top only to find myself at the bottom. Like Frank Sinatra, "I did it my way."

I am sure a psychiatrist or a psychologist friend of mine would have a field day with "The Boys" and their childhood or lack of it as the case may be. Yet I am not interested in their mumbo-jumbo. I have lived it, and now through the wisdom of the Holy Spirit, I am able to understand exactly how it affected the man I became.

My grandfather taught me how to work, he did not convey any joy in work, it was simply something one did to survive, not enjoy. Consequently I grew up always looking over the fence for something better, always looking for something more satisfying. I never seemed to find whatever it is, regardless of how hard I tried. Unfortunately, my grandfathers teaching included nothing about money. The result being I was always broke and deeply in debt, even at the height of my professional career. My rebellion, combined with fence hopping resulted in constant moves and new jobs.

As I grew up the desire of my heart was to go to sea. I strongly wanted to make a career in the military, especially the US Coast Guard. My wish was to attend the Coast Guard Academy and have a career at sea. Rebellion caused me to quit school in the ninth grade and join the US Air Force instead.

Rebellion also effected my relationships with others in fueling my constant search for love and approval. This, combined with the fact I had not a clue about love or intimate relationships, I had many relationships and marriages over the years. All of which ended because of my continual search for something better, someone new and more exciting. I simply did not know how to be faithful or loving, let alone a companion. I cobbled together an idea over the years, I am not completely without intelligence, but, I could never figure out the "how part." The resulting consequence being, there was always something missing, all were doomed from the beginning.

I have four children by two different mothers all are grown adults living in the southwest part of the country, many miles and borders away from me. They all have children the youngest being in their middle teens. There are also a scattering of grandchildren and even one or two great grandchildren. I see them infrequently for a large number of reasons. Mostly though, because I still after all these years, seventy since my fathers death, have a great deal of difficulty maintaining relationships. Do I love my children? I would say yes, but ask me what that means and I cannot say, so we remain distant.

Now here I am this deeply flawed individual, essentially not so different from most of you, but flawed none the less. Since I came to the Lord in August 1980, I wish I could say all of this was changed miraculously, it was not. Yet some how with all my faults and inconsistencies I was still told, **"Build My boat and preach My word, preach My word and build My boat."**

THE GIVING OF DEBORAH

How does a man tell of the woman with whom he lives day in and day out? I have written that I never learned how to love and given some of those details. It is a life long affliction. Yet, there is also the need for relationship, and between a man and a woman there is always that strain and tension which has existed from the beginning origins. Ever since Adam replied to God, as he hid in his nakedness, "The woman you gave to me," that tension exists.

All I know, is that from the moment Debbie was introduced into my life, my efforts consist mainly of returning to her presence. That is, regardless of our current temper, if we are separated by work, travel, or whatever, all I want is to be back together. I am hooked as it is said. I do not know, it must be love. Debbie became and is such an integral part of the story of S/V MARANATHA that I must tell of her here. I believe without her this story would not exist.

I have told in a previous chapter I met Debbie one evening after church over "rubber soup." Although she was an attractive woman in her mid thirties, she most definitely was not my type. Top that off with the fact that I was not looking. I left the Sizzler that evening secure in the belief that I had once again escaped from the clutches of grasping females. I never gave Debbie a second thought, for it was the other woman present that evening whom I was congratulating myself for escaping. The Lord, however, seems to have had other plans.

As I later learned, Debbie also never gave me a second thought, for her life was essentially in the same state as mine. She had gone through her struggles with marriage and relationships and now in the summer of 1984 found herself quite content with her single status. Her only lover was the Lord, in this she was secure and satisfied.

Debbie was very active at our church. She spent her Sunday mornings working as the assistant director of the Children's Sunday school, the reason she was not very active in the adult singles group. She worked at a fine dining restaurant, the "Velvet Dove", and was a full time collage student. She did not have a lot of empty time on her hands.

Debbie enjoys a very close relationship with the Lord which manifests itself differently than mine, but that is the way it should be, since we are different people and need different direction. Debbie takes the Lord everywhere she goes and consults Him as to everything, every daily decision, large or small.

"The Lord's so good," she told me shortly after our second meeting, "He even helps me pick out my toilet tissue."

Read that statement again. This is a real walk with the Lord! Most of us keep the Lord in reserve for the big hard decisions of life. We only consult Him when we are faced with real tough challenges which we cannot solve. We chose to take care of the small stuff ourselves. We do not realize as we do this we are missing out on a true intimate relationship with the Lord. The kind of intimacy that only comes from spending time with each other sharing the small stuff. We just blunder on handling, not consulting, relegating our Lord to a position of silence, pushed into the background of our lives. Is it any wonder when we do finally call on Him it takes so long for Him to answer? He has been excluded so long and so thoroughly that if He speaks to us at all, His answer just might be "I never knew you."

Debbie had learned if she included the Lord in everything she did, even the selection of her toilet tissue, there could never be any distance between her and her Lord whom she loves more that life. He is always right beside her ready to "handle the important stuff." He is our Lord, and when He promised to live for us He meant that exactly. We are the ones who decided He is too large for the small details, not Him. Large objects are built from small details.

Shortly after our first meeting I was returning home earlier than usual one evening. The sail boat races had been canceled due to weather, my friend and I had put the boat up in disgust and headed for home. I decided to stop off at a "Sizzler" on the south side, close to my apartment. I had not eaten and was in no mood to cook for myself. As I worked my way through the line, I was surprised to see Debbie, sitting at a table deeply involved in conversation with another Lady. My surprise was due to the fact that I knew her to be a "north-sider", north and south usually never mixed in Oklahoma City. I found a table, put my tray down and went over to her table just to be polite.

"Hello, what are you doing on this side of town?" she asked.

"I live over here, just two or three blocks down the road. What are you doing here? I thought you were a north-sider?" I said.

"I go to school at South Oklahoma City Junior Collage and my classes let out early so I stopped to have a bite and visit with a friend." She said.

We exchanged a few more meaningless, but pleasant words and I went back to my table and food. Neither of us gave a thought to how we had both ended up in the same restaurant some thirty miles from our first meeting and the church which was our only common ground. I must admit though, I did not return to my table as free of this woman as I had from our first meeting. Something in my spirit told me everything had changed.

It was early June and as I had planned earlier I moved back to the north side to an apartment closer to my church. I never gave Debbie any thought, yet I some how knew I was moving into a new phase of life. I was excited to be moving back to the north side and the new life this would mean for me. Events which took place over the next few months puzzle me to this day.

Neither Debbie nor I were looking for a mate or a relationship of any kind, yet every time we turned around, there was the other one. Usually we would find ourselves paired off in situations where we would have long conversations about the Lord, our lives and experiences with

Him. But I never shared the vision or its circumstances. Possibly it was too private, or maybe I just did not what her to think I was a nut. I do not know.

That summer was a particularly active time socially at our church with many church sponsored activities. Though it was not my habit, I found myself going to these functions and there she would be, and somehow we would wind up the evening together in deep conversation.

The church sponsored a Forth of July celebration that year which was a rather large affair with live entertainment including Phil Driscole and others, picnics, fire works, watermelon, all the traditional Independence Day ingredients. The day was to start early and last well into the night. A huge crowd was expected as our church at the time boasted some five thousand members and with guests, and the curious, attendance was expected to top eight thousand. Debbie had made a point to ask if I would be there and I had assured her I would, however, we made no plans to meet.

My daughter Amanda and I had started early that day, preparing our picnic and departed early for the church grounds hoping to find a good parking spot and a reasonably good spot to spread our picnic from which to enjoy the day.

We arrived around noon and already the grounds were fairly crowded. We set up our blanket and picnic in what seemed to be the perfect spot. But something was not right, Mandy and I looked at each other and agreed we should move. Several moves later we were located on a small rise close to the parking lot, under a large post oak tree, next to a side walk with a good view and breeze, if any stirred.

No sooner had I got settled in then I heard a voice say, "Hi." it was Debbie of course. She had parked her car not far away and out of thousands of people had walked straight to us. "Looks like your all set up. I'm going to try and find a place down on the field so I can hear Phil Driscole better. Enjoy yourselves!" She said. She said hello to Mandy whom she had met once or twice and made her way down the hill disappearing into the crowd.

To say she disappeared is not the truth, for from that moment to this, Debbie has never left my sight. As I originally wrote these words some years ago, I was in the middle of the Gulf of Mexico and I had not seen Debbie for several weeks, but she had never left my sight. As I rewrite these words today nothing has changed for even when we are apart for whatever reason she never leaves my sight.

That day as she turned away and started down the hill the Lord spoke to me in that wonderful voice I knew so well, **"I have given this woman to be your wife. Love her and cherish her as you do me."** At that moment He placed within me love for Debbie so deep I was riveted to the spot. A condition foreign to a being who did not know how to love, still did not, yet the Lord does. I could not take my eyes off her, nor, could I move for several minutes.

August 1, 1984 Kenneth D. Linnell, the first born of Kenneth and Inola Linnell and Deborah Ann Pollard, first born of Thomas and Ruth Pollard, were married in the club house of my new apartment complex, much to the joy and rejoicing of some, and the consternation of others. Some, many in fact, mostly those of the mature singles set of our church proclaimed, "it would never last," and who knows they might be right. As of this coming August 1, 2015, the marriage will have lasted only thirty one years, and it is not over yet, so they may yet be proven correct.

PART II

NO FRILLS NO THRILLS

I stood in the dark facing east. The night was very dark since there was no moon and thin low clouds dampened the light of the stars. Far in the distance, at regular intervals, a pinpoint of light would break through the blackness, that light was our goal.

It was January 7, 1985, approximately 3am and I was standing on the deck of a large four masted schooner as we sailed an easterly course into the Atlantic swells. We were sailing towards the Island of St. Barts. One of the Leeward Islands of the Lesser Antilles located on the boundaries of the Atlantic ocean and the Caribbean sea south southeast of the Florida coast of the United States.

We had departed the Island of St. Kitts, another of the leeward islands, around 6 pm the evening before anticipating arrival at St. Barts around 8 am the following morning. The exact time of our arrival was unknown, for as Captain John had said in his very British accent, "we'r a sailing vessel you know!"

It was to be our last night under sail and I not wishing to miss a moment of it had spent the night on deck, wedged into the starboard rail near the main mast at a point where the shrouds descended from the darkness and joined the hull out board of the rail. I spent the night with the rhythmical rise and fall of the ship as she met the swell entering the Caribbean from the Atlantic. The official boundary between these two bodies of ocean was just a few miles east of our position, however someone had forgotten to inform the Atlantic swell that it was trespassing upon the peace and tranquility of its smaller neighbor.

I listened to the sound of the wake as it slipped along the side of the vessel. The creak of the rigging overhead as the wind filled the sails drum tight and as the swell worked the rig, it all added to the mesmerizing effect of the night. I stood there unaware of the time. I was where I belonged, on the deck of a sailing vessel at sea, far from the modern world, transported to another time.

That night was a bench mark moment in my life, a night to which I returned many times through the years. That night remains as fresh and clear as the night I lived it. Many times the recalling of that night has kept me going, when everything around me told me to give up and quit!

JOURNEYS

"What are you going to be doing during Christmas break?" I asked Debbie, my bride of four or so months.

"I don't know, what are you going to do?" She countered.

"Well, I thought I'd spend most of it in the Caribbean, sailing among the islands, getting a tan and watching the pretty girls. Got any idea what you are going to be doing during the break yet?" I stated in a rather self satisfied manner.

"Debbie looked at me rather coolly, something she has always done rather well, and stated flatly, "I haven't a clue what you are talking about, but whatever you've got up you sleeve you can believe I am going to be wherever you are during Christmas! Now are you going to tell me what's going on or not?" In the four or so months since our wedding many changes had taken place in our lives, however Debbie had not yet learned to appreciate my sense of humor, it is possible she never has.

"Well if you insist," I said. "You and I are going on a tour of the islands to spy out the land. We have reservations to fly out of Miami the morning of December 31, to the island of St. Martin. We will meet our boat, The S/V Polynesia, there and then we will sail through some of the islands of the leewards and spy out part of our mission grounds. We will fly back to Miami on the 9th of January. We have to drive to Miami because all the flights out of anywhere close to Oklahoma City are all booked solid with people going to the Orange Bowl. The University of Oklahoma was once again playing the Orange Bowl this year, so the only way for us to make our connections is to drive to Miami, and enjoy the sights as we go. How's that sound for something to do during Christmas break?"

Silence! She just stood there propped up by the kitchen counter, looking at me as if I had lost my mind.

"I think you need to tell me the rest of the story," she said, "I've got a few questions that need answers. So start talking buster, this trip your talking about is less than two weeks from now, so fill me in on the details." My bride has ever been one to look a gift horse in the mouth.

—∞◦◦◦❊◦◦◦∞—

I have stated earlier, the vision the Lord started for me in early 1982 has never missed a day since its beginning moments, however, there are times when the intensity is not as strong. I suppose this could be because I have simply grown accustomed to living with the pictures on a constant daily basis. However, it is these times of relative inactivity which give me a chance to rest up for the more intense sessions, so perhaps they are intentional after all.

The vision process was in one of those low level periods during the spring of 1984, this had allowed me to meet and marry Debbie, and possibly contributed to the omission of my not telling her about the visions or the my call to ministry. Over the years I have convinced myself, that the reasons for this rather large omission was that I had met someone who genuinely liked me, even loved me. Someone who wanted to be with me and in one of my more grand moments of intelligence, I had managed to fool her into marrying me, and I did not want her to run off screaming into the hills when she discovered I was totally bollixing bonkers.

In another of my grander moments of intelligence, I determined to ignore all I had gone through prior to meeting Debbie and decided that the visions etc. could just be ignored and she would never be the wiser. As I have said, I am a very wise person, I also seem to never learn.

The day after our wedding the Lord cranked up the intensity dramatically. The intensity was so great I was totally distracted, everyone except Debbie, thought my distraction was just due to my newly wed status, and I took a lot of ribbing on that subject. Debbie became concerned that I was unhappy or disappointed with her, a not unusual conclusion for a new bride. I must admit I did not handle her reaction properly. My distraction was so complete, I forgot she knew nothing of the process, so commandingly displayed before me. Also, by this time I had become extremely fearful I could not conceal all of this from her, and I did not want her to know she had married a raving lunatic. I must here state, that now after almost thirty years of marriage, Debbie has become resolved if not reconciled to the apparent fact of her husbands lunacy. I finally realized I must tell her while there remained a chance of convincing her she was not my problem.

One evening during our first week of marriage I asked her to sit with me at the table as I had something I must tell her. Over the next several hours I told her the whole story. I told of my time in the hospital, the call of ministry, and the visions, of my seclusion and my return. I explained in great detail the visions and how they work, also the varying intensities, Everything I could possibly think of to correct my mistake of not telling her before our marriage. I felt very bad about not telling her a lot sooner. I explained how the intensity had been very low for sometime when I met her and in the excitement surrounding our coming together I had almost forgotten about it all. I even felt it possible that it was all over for I still did not take the whole thing very serious as I saw very little way any part of this amazing program would ever take place.

As I remember Debbie sat quietly as I told her my story, understanding more I think than I, how all this was to affect our lives from that moment forward.

I told her about the visions increasing to full and demanding intensity the day following our wedding. Now included in with the never ending detail, was a new element, now there was a date to begin construction. Construction of the S/V MARANATHA was to begin during the first half of the month of Adar, an ancient Jewish month roughly corresponding to February-March of our current calendar. I had not been given a specific year, however, I was strongly impressed with a sense of urgency and a need to not be lax about this requirement.

In Prayer I had asked many times for clarification of the time and my only answer was, "the time is now"!

Debbie absorbed all of this and sat there looking me for sometime. She did not as I had feared run screaming for the hills or even berate me for not telling her earlier, when she still had a chance to escape me, instead she simply said, "What do you think your supposed to do now?"

"I do not know", I answered, "I suppose if I am going to be some kind of minister I should go to school somewhere to learn more than I do now about ministry or whatever."

After some discussion on that point, we decided I should investigate a Bible School we had heard of through some friends, to see where that might lead. Secondly, we agreed the first step to any building program was to develop a set of drawings or plans from which the vessel in the vision could be built at some future date. We then went about our newly wedded lives, adjusting to each other, certain we were doing our best to answer the call presented by these insistent visions. The visions increased in intensity and detail to full panoramic vision with surround sound and daily the deadline of Adar became stronger. A fact of life which was not to be missed.

Within a few weeks time I was enrolled at the Bible School our friends had told us about. I attended classes four mornings per week and spent afternoons and evenings at the office or in the field. All was proceeding well except for my partner Gerald who couldn't resist calling me on my beeper, prior to cell phones, during class. I finally just left the thing in my truck which drove him straight up a tree. Debbie was immersed in her studies full time, since our wedding she did not work outside the home, her full time job was her school.

The search for plans had gone through several gradual evolutions. We had contacted several marine architects and plan services, explaining the vessel required to each in turn. After many lengthy conversations and dead ends we realized they, either could not or would not, design a vessel to fit the one in the vision. Those who indicated some interest suggested a price for their efforts in excess of $6,000.00 for the initial drafting and design work, with additional charges if additional changes were required. Needless to say this did not fit within our budget.

After sometime I remembered reading about a small sailing vessel designed in the late 1920's by John Hanna. The plans had recently been redrawn and made available to DYI boat builders at a price below $100.00 which was affordable. At 22ft over all this boat was too small for our requirements, however, it did fit the general hull style and rig of the vessel in the vision. I sent for the plans and after studying the drawings realized that by increasing the size of the hull it would fit perfectly with the MARANATH of the vision. The deck structures and internal layout would be added to the hull drawings with ease once the offsets, a term describing dimensions in marine architecture, were scaled up to the larger vessel size.

I began to draw the lines and calculate the offsets in early October and slowly but surely the shape of a forty two foot vessel began to take shape. I labored over the plans daily until in early December I considered the lines and offsets of the hull complete. This had not been an easy task. The drafting part was relatively simple due to my training as an architect, but the calculations for the curved lines and structural dimensions required to attain their shape had been most difficult to produce.

One of the small details the Lord had failed to include in His very detailed visions, was the exact size of the vessel I was to build. Unlike my brother, Noah, I had no dimensions stated in cubits or otherwise. This really turned out for the good since I have no idea what a cubit is and calculations in good old feet and inches were difficult enough. Yet for the detail of specific dimensions I was on my own.

I had arrived at an over all length of between forty to fifty feet through research and knowledge of the most comfortable size for sailing, sea keeping, and ground tackle size for a short handed crew. The forty two foot size had emerged as the easiest dimension for the overall increase of the purchased plans, requiring the fractions contained within the results and therefore the least complicated to draft and subsequently construct. At least so I thought in my grand intelligence mentioned earlier.

So by December of 1984 I had the beginnings of a set of plans and I was satisfied I was doing all I could do to meet the insistent requirement to begin construction in the month of Adar or mid February to mid March of 1985. Elsewhere our lives were progressing as normally as possible I suppose. The demands of school and business on both Debbie and I were no greater or less than others in similar circumstances. There was not a lot of free time remaining in any day. We stayed out of trouble and enjoyed our lives.

In mid September, short weeks after our wedding, Debbie and I finally felt a release from our bound to our church. We had moved to a new church and were enjoying the experience of new freedom's of the Holy Spirit which operated there and the making of new friends. Strangely enough our departure from our old church had provided Debbie and I with legitimacy in the eyes of those who had attempted hardest to destroy us.

We received many invitations to attend and speak, minister as some put it, at various gatherings of the adult singles group conducted off the campus of the church. I suppose the story of our romance had become a prime example of the old saw, "even a blind dog will catch a rabbit once." However, with one or two acceptations, and only on a one to one basis, we kept our distance from our old church for the next few years.

Debbie had accepted the visions as part of life with her "crazy" new husband, yet, they did not carry the same importance nor urgency for her as they did for me. Over the years I have finally come to realize this to be a normal condition.

This is a fact of being called, all who are called must realize and work within, or the road of calling will be difficult in the least and doomed to failure and strife in the worst. Those around us, especially our loved ones and closest associates, will support us in whatever we do, but they will not have the same drive as the one who is called. Likewise those who are not to be described as loved ones or close associates will attach themselves to the calling in the vain hope to vicariously live their own envisioned calling through your call, and if allowed will change and tarnish the vision, possibly again to the point of failure and destruction.

I made the error as I believe most of us who are called to specific and insistent visions make. I expected my bride of a few short months, one who had known of the "project" but a very short time, to carry within her the same enthusiasm for the project as I. I wonder at the grandness of my intelligence at times, substitute stupidity.

God may at times give them a word for you, and they through their love for you will tolerate your devotion to the vision, but you are the one who is called. You are the one who is driven to accomplish whatever task the Lord has given. Those around you may be willing workers, but do not expect them to be as focused as yourself.

Until I learned this particular peculiarity of God's call upon the called, I created a lot of difficulties for myself. I must admit I still feel more than a little frustration when others do not seam to catch the fever of the visions and ministry as strongly as I. At least I now have some small clue as to why they are as they are. I suppose the frustration is another problem I have to work out. Oh well, to paraphrase my friend John Wesley, of Methodist fame, the road to perfection is long and perfection while attainable in this life for the believer, the attainment of that perfection in this mortal realm is highly unlikely.

On the numerous occasions we discussed the mission, Debbie, would flatly state that I would just have to wait for God's timing. This was a very popular statement at the time, as I am sure it may still be. I place it in the category of excuse for doing nothing, and on a similar scriptural status as the infamous passage from First Benny chapter one verse one, "The Lord helps those who help themselves."

It drove me crazy and still does. What my beloved bride did not see was that I had God's timing, it was now or very soon to be now. And unless I could figure out the how of the now, I would miss the mark. At the time I had no answer for her statement, I seemed to be unable to convey the sense of urgency building in my spirit. She was not burdened as was I with the certain knowledge that construction of the MARANATHA must begin with the up coming month of Adar. This was not a request but a command.

Consider the foundations of my frustration with this "command", or what to me and I am sure to my bride also, was the impossibility of the situation. We lived comfortably, but there were no extra funds, we owned no property and had no prospect of raising the funds required to launch a major construction project. Who in their right mind was going to give money to a modern day Noah to build a sea going sailing vessel in the middle of Oklahoma, USA?

We had no tools, no place to build a large boat, and how could we be expected to accomplish a project such as this in several years, let alone start in just a few short months? It is no wonder Debbie would not take the whole thing seriously, and at the least, she probably believed I was trying to force things to happen in my own way.

For my own part I was as frustrated with the impossibility as Debbie. The primary difference being that I had the sense of urgent command growing in my spirit knowing it must be done. I knew somehow, in this one thing at least, failure was not an option, Yet, at every turn there was nothing with which to proceed, I just had to keep on keeping on.

Add to all this pressure, for several weeks I had a growing feeling that there was something I was to do, some task to be accomplished before all this was to begin in Adar, a few short weeks away. I had no idea what it could be and answers never came in prayer, at least none that helped. Only the constant reply of **"Build my boat and preach my word, preach my word and build my boat."** I was just aware of some act I was to preform, some requirement which must be settled before construction of MARANATHA could begin. As if there were not details enough to settle.

So, added into the mix with all the rest, I was constantly on the look out for whatever to come along. One morning in mid December I was in the final class of the morning at Bible School. Pastor Roger was leading us through the book of Nehemiah, bringing to life the story and scriptures as only he could. We were studying the portion of the story where Nehemiah after returning to Jerusalem walks among the ruins of the city to spy out the land. As I contemplated these scriptures and this story, suddenly the Lord spoke to me in that voice I know so well, **"This I would have you do. Go into the islands of the sea and spy out the land."**

At that moment I knew the thing which had evaded me for weeks. I knew we had to go as soon as possible and with Christmas break being less than two weeks distant, this seemed to be the perfect time. I also knew our trip must include the island of Nevis.

During the balance of the class I sat there with my mind ablaze with what had just happened and with more than one question as to how this was to be accomplished. The test of the veracity of this revelation would be to make all the required arrangements without hassle or complications or stress so close to the holiday season. If I could make reservations, confirm bookings, etc., not to mention find the funds to pay for such a venture, on such short notice it all had to be "of God".

I arrived at my office that day about 12:30pm. I immediately called a travel agent I knew, and gave her the requirements of the itinerary. She promptly informed me of the utter impossibility of such a task on such short notice at that particular time of the year. I asked that she try, and she reluctantly agreed to attempt the impossible. As I placed the phone back in its cradle, ancient days these, I thought, "Well if this is what God wants it will fit together."

One hour later my friend called. "I don't really know how it happened", she stated, "but I can book you on a Wind Jammer cruise beginning at St. Marrten for the dates you need which will visit seven islands in as many days, one of them being Nevis. You will have to drive to Miami as there are no seats available due to Orange Bowl traffic. You will stay one night on St. Marrten at the end of the cruise as the return flight to Miami is only once a week, and that is the day after your cruise ends. I have a hold on a room at the KLM hotel on the French side of St. Marrten/Martin pending your approval. I am really surprised all this is available at this late date."

"You are sure Nevis is on the itinerary?" I asked.

"Yes, I made certain their agent understood Nevis must be included. They assured me it was," she stated.

"OK, make the arrangements and let me know when I can pick up the tickets," I said.

Thirty minutes later all the reservations had been made and funds had come available through my portion of the business to finance the trip. By 3:00pm that afternoon I had in my possession the airline tickets, hotel and cruise reservations, everything required to make our journey except the boarding passes for the boat in St. Marrten. The one thing lacking in this wonder of wonders was that my bride knew absolutely nothing about how I intended her to spend her Christmas break, I closed up my desk and hurried home.

ISLANDS, LITTLE BIRDS, SUNRISE, AND AMY GRANT

W_e arrived in the leeward Islands of the Lesser Antilles at 6:30 pm local time December 31,1984 Specifically the island of St. Marrten/ Martin one half being Dutch and one French, hence the duplicitous name designation. There are many details I will passover about our days spent in the islands. Though they were few, the details of our journey that December/January could fill a book by themselves. Included here are only three anecdotes which I feel pertinent to the story of the S/V MARANATHA.

As soon as the hustle of boarding our ship, a four masted 210 ft schooner, was over we had time to think about where we were and the events taking place around us. Debbie and I were struck with a feeling of helplessness due to the enormity of it all. I was increasingly aware of a growing feeling of hopelessness as we traveled from island to island, meeting people, observing what was going on around us, learning of their past and hopes for the future. We were thousands of miles from home, we knew no one. We were not to actively witness, but to observe, and one fact seemed constantly before us, "How could we possibly do what God had told us to do?" We were only two people, true we had God on our side, but the ministry had suddenly taken on an immenseness which made it seem totally and utterly impossible. Ponder if you will the problem we faced. Two ordinary people of modest income, were to build a sailing vessel in the middle of the North American Oklahoma red clay prairie hills, then sail it thousands of miles to establish mission churches and programs throughout the islands of the sea. Who would not be over whelmed?

After several days and three or four islands I began to seriously ask the Lord if I had misunderstood Him, and I know Debbie was doing the same. During these days the Lord was strangely silent and our concern deepened. Frankly we were both half scared to death.

One afternoon we found ourselves on the Island of St. Christopher, St. Kitts to the locals, relaxing in an open air restaurant on the beach by Frigate Bay. Debbie and I had been discussing our day and our concern over the problems I have just outlined and our misgivings as to our ability to accomplish the overwhelming ministry assigned to us.

We grew silent as the waitress approached with our orders and I silently began to ask God for some sign that we were at least where we were supposed to be at the time. Doing what we were supposed to be doing.

As we began to eat, a little bird flew into the restaurant and landed on our table. It was a very small bird, black with a rust-orange breast, about the size of a canary. The waitress came to shoo it away and it flew around the room until she left our table and then the bird returned to us. Throughout the remainder of our time at the restaurant that afternoon the little bird remained with us. We fed it some sugar and some of our salad, and no matter who tried to shoo it away or lure it to another table it remained our luncheon companion and ours alone. I remember the bird never made a sound, but ate with us, looking us both directly in the eyes as though it were our own special friend. As I watched this little bird I knew I had the sign I had asked for moments earlier. My mood began to improve immediately and as I looked at my bride I realized she too had received more or less the same message as I from our very special luncheon companion.

Our little friend allowed us to get our cameras and posed for us as we took its picture several times. It quickly darted from side to side, tilting its head one way or the other as if to show off its fine little yellow beak. Lunch with our friend was a pure delight. As if on cue it knew it was time for us to go. It fluttered to a bush just outside of the low wall beside our table, turned, looked into both our faces for a long moment and flew away.

Debbie and I sat there in silence for a several minutes. We still had many questions and some apprehension, but now we both knew we were exactly where we were supposed to be at that moment in the history of the universe.

We both were overwhelmed that our Lord had sent such a beautiful luncheon companion, especially to us.

We enjoyed the remainder of our day and gave no more thought to the ministry and all its cogent problems, real or imagined. We sailed from "St. Kitts" that evening and enjoyed several rainbows playing over the island and the harbor as rain squalls moved from the Caribbean to the Atlantic.

We thoroughly enjoyed the evening as we sailed around St. Kitts toward the island of St. Barts, and I remember enjoying each other, really for the first time during the trip. I cannot fully explain how a little black bird, with it's rusty orange breast and bright yellow beak could have such an effect upon us. It simply had to be the Lord! That event has provided me with one of the most pleasant memories of my wife and the islands.

As Debbie retired for the evening I found myself unable to sleep. I returned to the weather, upper, deck and wedged myself in along the starboard rail and began the vigil described at the opening of this section.

It was then during this vigil as I watched the seas and the bow waves flow alongside the ship that the Lord broke His silence. He began to reveal details of the visions and its connected ministry, previously until this moment hidden, and unknown to me. He brought back many details which I had forgotten and while He was at it He refreshed the call and my anointing.

Among many things which happened that evening was one of most startling consequence, speaking to me in that most wonderful of voices, my Lord and friend, rather casually said to me, "**Son the boat you have designed is too small.**" I was dumb founded, I had labored for months over the plans and the only thing He could say was "it's too small!" How about something like,"I really like what you have done and I really appreciate all the hard work you have done getting the design ready." Any praise for my efforts would have been appropriate, at least that is what I thought as I stood there with my jaw on the deck. However, all I got was, "its too small." The Lord really knows how to put me in my place! I think I could have accepted it being the wrong boat design easier that it simply being too small.

"What do you mean too small?" I cried in frustration. "Just how big is it supposed to be?" "And I must say you have been silent on this point up to this moment and you have left it till pretty darned late in the game if I do say so!"

"**Sixty feet overall with a cargo hold amidships, and berth space for a crew of six,**" came the answer. "And just when, am I supposed to have all this started?" I shot back more than a little miffed.

"**When you return to your home. Then in the month of Adar you must begin the building of the vessel MARANATHA.**" Then silence, broken only by the motion of the ship as it moved through the wind and the waves. I stood wedged in at the rail in the silence of a sailing vessel at sea, shell shocked! How could I do this thing now? I had just been informed that the plans I had spent weeks and weeks preparing were essentially useless. At least the most important part, the offsets or construction dimensions, were now of no use what so ever. Everything, now had to be recalculated and redrawn, and by my reckoning the month of Adar was now just something less than six weeks distant. Standing there I was consumed with just one monumental question, "Just how in the devil was I supposed to do this now?"

At the height of my frustration dawn began to break, I stood there watching as a glorious sun inched over the Atlantic swells, and the Lord spoke to me once more.

"**My son, consider the sun rising. Sunset is beautiful and I fill it with glory and wonders, but it is an ending followed by the darkness. Sunrise is filled with glories of it's own for it is new life,**

life not yet lived or filled with the cares and worries of the day. My son just as the sun rises over these islands of the sea, I have given you a new song for My Son in the islands of the sea."

How can I describe my feelings at this point? I had been angry at being under appreciated by God and had been on the verge of telling Him off quite strongly. Possibly telling Him to go fly a kite and get someone else to carry out this "cock-a-mamie" scheme. Then He goes and tells me something like this. My heart was broken and I wept and wept. The sun rise was I believe the most beautiful I had ever witnessed.

Even now as I am on watch in the early morning as the sun rises, pushing away the false dawn with its brilliance, I recall the promise made to me once so many dawns ago. While I am at sea the sunsets are most always beautiful with nothing but the horizon and the water to compliment God's paintings. Sun rise is special for me, it comes always with its promise of new beginnings, new life and new songs to be sung to the glory our our Lord! I wrote this section originally while I was an active Captain working for an oilfield supply company among the oil fields in the Gulf of Mexico.

That beautiful sunrise coupled with its message held me transfixed. Only moments before I was on the verge of throwing in the proverbial towel, overwhelmed with the impossibility of it all, then suddenly the Lord! What else can be said but, *"Suddenly the Lord."* How could I resist? As the sun rose steadily I went below to tell Debbie of my night at sea and the events which had transpired.

We spent the balance of the day enjoying each other and the island of St. Barts and that evening we sailed, our last night at sea, and morning found us anchored in the harbor off Phillipsburg, St. Marrten. We departed the vessel and journeyed across the island to the French side where we were to spend the day and night prior to our flight to Miami the next morning.

———◦◦◦❦◦◦◦———

One of the American luxuries we had left behind while on our excursion around the islands of the Lesser Antilles, was hot water, hot showers or baths seem to be for the most part very rare. So as we checked into the KLM hotel we were both eagerly looking forward to our first hot shower since leaving the hotel in Ft. Myers, Florida over a week distant. Hot water, was considered a given to Debbie and I, especially due to the cost of our room. We were escorted through the large open air lobby along a lovely curving path which followed the lovely tropical lagoon surrounded by palm trees and flowers. Our room turned out to be a secluded bungalow facing the beach, and lagoon, nestled in its own grove of palms. It was all something straight out of "Fantasy Island." We half expected "Tattoo or Mr. Rork" to appear at any moment, to put our fantasy adventure into motion.

The room though small was comfortable and contained the usual hotel accommodations, except the beds were two very narrow mattresses fastened securely to concrete block foundations, not the most comfortable in the world. We quickly investigated the shower, making plans for a relaxing hot shower. Just as quickly we discovered, not only was the water not hot it was not potable either. So once more we enjoyed cold showers, proving the local saying, "der be no 'ot waateer in de i'lan's mon!" to be all to true.

The next morning as we were preparing to to leave, we discovered both of us were very reluctant to return home. This was not the usual "end of vacation blues." But something much stronger and intense. Debbie and I both wanted to stay and work among the people of these islands. We were "here now," why return, why delay, why not right now? I know, had there been any alternative presented that morning, we would not have departed the islands, but would have stayed to begin the work then and there.

We went into the lobby area and told the desk clerk to call our taxi for the airport and then entered the open air restaurant to indulge in a most luxurious continental breakfast. There were mountains of breads, fruits, eggs and breakfast meats, along with gallons of juice, milk and coffee. Breakfast made up for the cold shower.

The restaurant was really only an extension of the lobby. It was all open and looking out over the beautiful lagoon. As we sat eating our breakfast the hotel pa system was tuned to a local radio station.

Contrasting to the view and the sumptuous meal the speaker directly overhead was screeching very non musical thumping's of hard rock recordings, a tuneless and remorseless din for 7:00am. "I don't know if I'm up to that this early in the morning." I said to Debbie with a smile. "It does ruin the mood of this beautiful place." She replied. We finished our meal, all the while being jarred by the noise coming from the overhead speaker.

We crossed the lobby, collected our luggage and reminded the desk clerk of our call for a taxi. We found a place by the entrance to await our ride to the airport. We stood there talking about our feelings of wanting to stay, knowing we must return home. We were still very reluctant to return to Oklahoma. All this time we were ignoring to the best of our ability the screeching coming from the speaker directly over our heads.

Suddenly, in the middle of a tune, or what passed for a tune, the screeching voice of the rock singer stopped, and much to our amazement, Amy Grant began to sing "El Shaddai." We stood there with our mouths open, listening to the beautiful stirring words of worship as Amy sang the song.

> El Shaddai, El Shaddai
> El El-yon na Adonai;
> age to age you're still the same
> by the power of the name.

When the last note was sounded, there was a moment of silence as if the whole world had its head bowed, as did Debbie and I. Then the rock noise resumed right where it had been interrupted. The DJ nor anyone in the hotel made any reference to what had just happened. Not one person in the hotel appeared to be aware the music had been interrupted and that God had been worshiped and praised.

Debbie and I looked at each other to confirm that we both had heard Amy sing that wonderful song. At that moment it was all right to leave these beautiful islands for the prairies of Oklahoma. We departed with the sure and certain knowledge that we were surrounded by the presence of "El Shaddai."

MID-AMBLE

A preamble as you know is a device by which a writer can set the stage for the story to follow while explaining certain facts pertinent to the writing of the story. Not being a writer, I shall take advantage and invent a segment at this point. Before I continue with the story of MARANATHA there are certain things which I feel require explanation or some calcification, therefore, I have invented the

"Midamble."

This seems to be the proper point at which to state the purposes for writhing this story. As well as the time for the telling of some other facts, so as to invest the reader with knowledge required to understand some of the events and reactions to them, which were to take place in Debbie's and my lives during the next few years.

My purpose in committing our story to the written word is two fold, first, it was meant to be and has become a sort of healing process for me. The reader will discover some events which were very difficult for me to relive, and betrayal by trusted friends, brothers, and associates. These events were very arduous for me to understand and forget. I began the telling of this tale hoping to place these events in the past, and as I have proceeded it has become evident that the working through these times in Debbie's and my lives was one of the purposes the Lord had in mind for me as I tell this story. Secondly it is my hope to reach those who are called to ministry, especially those who are called to a ministry which does not fit into the often narrow minded prescribed version of ministry as currently understood in today's world of the church-ed.

It is my hope that by the telling of my tale, those called by God will be able to miss some of the land mines placed in their paths, as they travel on their course toward the completion of their own given vision. The land mines I speak of are not placed there by the enemy of our Lord, or his henchmen, though there will be plenty of those and they are never ceasing. These are easily recognizable. As Spirit led Christians we can or should easily deal with them, as they are detonated in our face, and go victoriously along our way. Christ has already given us the victory over anything the enemy attempts, therefore, for those who are in Christ, nothing the enemy works against us has any power. The only power the enemy has to work his destruction is that which we give to him.

The land mines I am most concerned with are those placed in our paths by our fellow Christians and co-laborers, and even by ourselves. Because we as mortals have finite minds we have difficulty accepting the truth of our standing and position as heirs with Christ, and we judge ourselves by the reactions of our fellow Christians. We use their reactions and judgments to and of ourselves, our actions, our work, in effect our lives, as the yard stick by which our health and growth are measured.

This is devastating and destructive when you find yourself surrounded by those you love and trust, but who are determined to force you to conform to their image of "whatever" so as to make you fit within their particular "God box." This is the danger contained within a finite mind, theirs or yours, when that mind decides it knows all there is to know about God, and it then builds a box in which to hold Him. The problem is God never ever completely fits within the confines of the box so carefully constructed to hold Him. Consequently when someone comes along with a vision from God, who does not fit into that very carefully constructed "God box," that person cannot be accepted and the landmines are deployed. After all this person cannot be of God, they do not fit in the box. If an example of someone like this is needed, a person who did not fit in the box whom we all know, look no farther than Jesus of Nazareth.

People who profess to follow the same Lord as you, cheerfully cast hand grenades in your direction, while pressing the handle to detonate the landmines they have concealed under the ground upon which you stand. These problems are not as easily recognized or dealt with, for do not forget these are the very people we judge ourselves by and we tend towards disbelief in their case. They are our brothers and sisters, joint heirs with Christ, and they have nothing but our best interests at heart. Right?

We simply cannot believe our brothers and sisters would harm us in such fashion. The mines they use are not designed to kill, though that is often the case, but only to maim and disfigure, to force submission to their particular vision and the box within which, the vision and you must fit. If submission cannot be achieved, then extrication must follow, and you suddenly find yourself on the outside looking in, wondering what just happened. Your vision must fit into their vision and must conform, for if it does not you and your vision cannot be of God and must be removed form their communion. Over the past several years I have had several occasions to study this phenomena first hand. I have finally come to the conclusion these attacks are rooted in jealously and envy. I know these are strong words but I speak from the platform of experience. I still, however, have difficulty understanding how a fellow Christian can be envious of another believers ministry. Each of us are called to ministry of one type or another. I just do not know what there is to be jealous or envious of in another believers call.

My friend and pastor Lowrie has a tremendous call upon his life. Lowrie has had a beautiful ministry as a pastor within the United Methodist Church and as a chaplain with the US Air Force Reserve. He has served with grace and distinction both as pastor and as chaplain rising to Command Chaplin prior to retirement a few years ago. I at times find myself envious of his abilities and the calm mildness with which he seems to approach his ministry. The point is, this is Lowrie's ministry, his call, what good would it do for me to be jealous? God has given me my own set of abilities and manner with which to accomplish the task assigned to me, not Lowrie's. I could not do his job if I tried, so why would I want to impose my wishes upon him? How could I presume to tell him how to accomplish his mission? God called him, not me or anyone else, to that particular mission, provided him with the tools and abilities to accomplish it, and the responsibility for its accomplishment.

The same is true for each and everyone of us, we should, instead of getting in each others way, be praising God for the diversity he has given us. We should be praying for each other, standing in the gap against the enemy. We should be helping each to overcome the land mines and grenades of the enemy, instead of placing our own demanding conformity upon each other, demanding conformity or else.

God called me to a certain ministry and you to yours. We, you and I, are totally and independently responsible to God for the ministries given us. As the person called, you are charged of God to fulfill all the obligations of that call, you and you alone are to maintain its purpose and direction. You must keep it pure and unaltered by outside influences. God did not call your spouse, your friends, pastor, mother, or father, ***He called you!!!***

This is not to say, no other person will be involved in helping you with the work. There will be many who will be of invaluable help and service, as there have been in mine. However, you must remember, while they are called to help they are not the one called to responsibility for the vision. Remember you are the one called to that, it is "your vision," not theirs. You are the one God called to accomplish the work. You must guide it and protect it, or it will become "their work," and not that which God called you to do. Moses was called, Arron was given to assist, but Moses was the one responsible and the one who had to face down Pharaoh. Read on in that story and see what happened when Arron briefly took control of Moses' vision.

You must learn to discern between the types of help which will be offered. There will be those who come with a genuine offer of service. Those who have accepted the call from God to assist in the ministry as directed and to be submissive to the call you have been given. These, accept service as their ministry and are a joy to have present, as by their submission in service, they allow you to concentrate on building and growth. They will be of both long and short tenure, and I am sad to say also few in number.

Another type are those who come, and say all the right things along with all the correct buzzwords, but retain silent strings to service. One thing will give them away and I offer it in the hope others will be spared some of the problems I faced by not knowing about these people in advance. These folks will immediately begin, both overtly and covertly, attempting vigorously to alter the ministry goals and methods to fit their own desires.

If your call is to homeless orphans, you will suddenly find yourself being involved with homeless single mothers as well. On the surface this is a laudable thing and a needed ministry. However, this is not what you were called to do, and no matter how hard you work to accomplish your goals they will not be blessed, because you have allowed your call to be changed into something other than the original vision.

Someone, who for whatever reason attached themselves onto your ministry vision and thereby changed the ministry, perverted it if you will, into something which it was not meant for you to accomplish. The one who is called of God to do a particular thing must do that thing. They must protect that work and its vision from all who would pervert it, be it the enemy or Christian brother or sister alike.

Nehemiah was called by God and blessed as he returned to Jerusalem to rebuild. He succeeded only because he stood firmly against all his detractors. He resolutely caused the work to be accomplished in the order and fashion in which he had been instructed by God. He in other words answered his ministry call and protected it. Nehemiah executed "his ministry" according to the exact purpose to which he had been called. I believe had he allowed the inclusion of the smallest change by one of his "helpers" he most certainly would have failed. At the very least the reconstruction would have been delayed countless years while God rearranged events to allow His plan to be consummated.

Thirdly, there will be those who come offering help, at times seemingly bringing with them answers to fervent prayer, but demanding the direction or method currently in progress be changed or stopped. The reason for these changes will essentially be that whatever you are currently about or your method of accomplishing it cannot be "of God," because it simply does not fit into any pattern of religious work of which they can conceive. You have committed the most grievous sin of not fitting into their "God box."

Guard carefully against the latter two types of Christians. They always come well informed and with well articulated arguments, and it is easy for a person focused on the particulars of a vision to be deceived. You will always be overworked in ministry and in great need of help, however, all that is offered is not always right or good, and does not always have your best interests at heart. **"BEWARE"**.

Welcome all who come, with and in love, but remain steadfast. Do not be surprised when some, even most, depart in bitterness and anger because you are "too single minded," or "too dogmatic," stating as they rush for the door, "you cannot be of God."

In the beginnings of my career in ministry, and in particular the events of this story, I was naive enough to believe that because God had called me and I had accepted the call, the Christian world would recognize, accept and support me and my ministry. How wrong can a person be?

Do not be surprised when you finally declare yourself, to find yourself talking to deaf and unwilling ears. One of the difficulties with the Charismatic movement is that everyone has "a ministry." Therefore, how could God possibly tell someone to assist another ministry with, time, talent, and God forbid money. When confronted by a ministry asking for their help these are most often the words they speak, "I'm too busy with my own ministry, but I'll pray for you." The kiss of death!

Be patient brother those whom God has called to work with you in your particular vineyard are out there and are usually found where and when you least expect them.

Last, I would like to mention that I was told as I began this writing to be as honest as possible, to let the story be told as it happened no matter the cost. This I have with the help of the Holy Spirit, done and am doing to the best of my ability. I have of necessity left out some events and details, but I have left out nothing which the Spirit has led me to believe important to the comprehension of the story of the S/V Maranatha.

It is my hope and prayer, that any who read this will be better prepared than I, when confronted with their brothers and sisters in Christ, and the down and dirty details of life in ministry.

WE BEGIN

Debbie and I returned home and resumed our lives, or more truthfully attempted to resume our lives. We found, however, our lives had changed. We simply were not the same. We had been absent from our country and home only a short time, but we suffered a great deal of culture shock upon our return. We reacted as if we had been absent years instead of days. We watched ourselves very closely in order to not be judgmental of the excesses we now seemed to notice in our society and nation, even our fellow Christians, at almost every turn.

Upon arriving home and returning to work, I found it increasingly difficult to continue my business relationship. When I discovered our silent partner's deception over his portion of the tithe, I took immediate steps to either close him out or exit myself. In the end I sold my share of the business to a new investor, and used my portion to pay business and personal debts, and start a new venture I hoped and believed would fund the ministry, but I am ahead of the story.

Shortly after our return I had sat down at the drafting table and considered the 42 ft. vessel over which I had labored for weeks. I simply could not believe that after all my efforts the Lord had told me it was too small. I believed this particular design to be within my abilities to construct, but none the less, I sat about revising the scant-lings, a marine term for boat dimensions, to those of the enlarged vessel presented to me that morning at sea a short time before.

One hour later I had completed the drawings and offsets for the larger vessel. She would be 60 ft. over all, being 51.5 ft. on deck with an 8.5 ft bowsprit. She was to carry two masts being 51.5 ft from the main mast truck to the water line. She would carry 1487 sq. ft. of canvas in four sails. All this in one hour! I probably would have had it completed faster, but I simply could not draw any faster, and besides I broke the lead in my pencil twice. Later when we lofted the lines only one dimension was off and that only by one quarter of an inch.

I was increasingly aware of the approaching deadline, Adar. That word kept growing in my mind with the passing of each day. I grew very concerned because nothing had changed, except my business relationship, which steadily deteriorated. As that relationship grew worst, so did my ability to accomplish this thing at all, let alone within the parameters established by the month of Adar.

One afternoon in the middle of February, the beginning of Adar, I was in my office engaged in a very frank discussion with the Lord. Being the gentleman He always is He was politely allowing me to speak my piece.

"Lord, I told you I'd do this crazy ministry, but I can't do it with nothing! It's already the middle of February and I still don't have funds to build a boat. It'll take at least $50,000.00 to $60,000.00 dollars to do this thing. I don't have tools or a place to build, we have the plans, but big deal, without the rest they are just so much toilet paper. I need your help if I'm going to do this crazy thing. It's your deadline not mine, and from where I sit, Lord, you've dropped the ball!" I railed and railed, I was totally frustrated. Yet as I talked the certain knowledge that construction must begin soon steadily grew stronger.

Suddenly He spoke. It was an audible presence apart from myself. A voice and a presence I had come to know very well." **Start with that which you have been given. I have never given my servants what they need in advance. Consider My servants and start with that which you have been given."**

I was silent, dumbstruck is more accurate. How could I be anything else? I had just been told by the Lord Himself to stop my whining and complaining and get busy! I sat there and considered what I had been told. My mind was suddenly filled with memories of the great people of faith in the scriptures. Joseph, Moses, Nehemiah, Issac, Joshua, on and on. In every case I could recall, these people of faith, given their instructions from God, had simply stepped out in faith and begun their work with what they possessed at the time.

All else, their every need was provided as they went along, as it was required. Never in advance, always on time, just in time, never in excess. The requirement, the first requirement, the essential requirement, was that they began their task in the moment they existed, with that which they possessed, with certain knowledge the means to accomplish the task would be given.

I knew I must quit my grousing about and start immediately. Start with what I had on hand, trusting God to provide as required. Also I realized, possibly for the first time, that this was God's ministry and mission, not mine. It's success or failure was his problem not mine. My task in all this was simply to provide a willing body to preform the job and keep my mind and senses open to hear His instructions clearly.

The latter part I struggle with more or less constantly and make more mistakes than I care to admit. The mistakes are at times disastrous, but the Lord is faithful to correct my errors once they come to light. Changing them for good even if that good is only to learn not to do that thing again.

I looked around me taking stock of my situation with new eyes, positive eyes, I looked for what I had and how I could start. I decided the first step should be the opening of a bank account, which I did that very afternoon. It was opened with the staggering sum of $79.00 dollars, a figure which was to remain fairly constant for the months and years to come. No matter how much was spent or deposited we always seemed to have a balance very close to $79.00 dollars. I suppose, as I look back, that account must have been my first mistake, even though I have never figured that out for certain.

Second I decided to accept an offer for my share of the business for $13,000.00 dollars. I would retain a 20% interest and was also to remain as director of operations. All was arranged in short order and the funds thus made available allowed for the settlement of some personal obligations. The remaining funds allowed for the rental of a large building and the purchase of the first materials dedicated to the construction of the S/V Maranatha were purchased. The balance in our account remained at $79.00 dollars.

During the month of Adar, at 7:30 pm February 21, 1985, a small group of friends and associates gathered on a chilly evening in a rented building located on the north bank of the South Canadian river, on the edge of Cow Town, in the heart of Oklahoma City, Oklahoma. The breeze from the south west, a constant in Oklahoma, filled the air faintly of the stock yards and confined cattle.

We had gathered in this in auspicious place to dedicate the start of the S/V Maranatha and the founding of Spirit Wind Ministries. Together we sang praises to our Lord, and offered prayers of thanksgiving. We dedicated ourselves to the work we were to do in that place, and to the Lord for His purposes.

After the singing and praying were done the construction of the S/V Maranatha was begun with the construction of the lofting floor. This is a large flat smooth surface upon which the lines of the vessel are drawn to full size. This is done in order to make certain all the curves are fair and smooth. Then from these "faired" lines full size patterns of the various components of the vessels hull are made. Thus allowing the construction of those parts, which are then assembled into the completed hull of the vessel.

Those gathered with Debbie and I that evening assisted us in the beginning of this tool, which in this case consisted of a wood framed floor sixty feet long and eighteen feet wide, built over the existing concrete floor of the shop building. After everyone present had the opportunity to drive a nail or two partaking personally of the official beginning, we closed the evening with prayer, and then departed to our homes.

I realize it may not sound like much, yet, that evening and its small beginning represented a large commitment for Debbie and I. As we departed for home that evening everything we had, physically, emotionally, and financially lay within the confines of that rather dirty, slightly smelly, ugly building on the south side of Oklahoma City. We were excited as we drove home that evening, knowing we had made personal commitments only the Lord could honor, not the least of which was the monthly rental on an 8000 sq, ft. building We felt, and I believe justifiably so, that we had given everything possible to the beginning of this ministry and we were looking forward to what God had planned for us next. The bank balance was $79.00 dollars.

If we would of had any idea of the coming events, that were to surround us in the coming year, I am certain this story would end now. However, the Lord in His mercy never revels more than we need to know at the moment. I think that might just be the definition of faith.

That night snuggled peacefully in our bed Debbie and I were blissfully ignorant.

DISTRACTIONS

If you have answered a call on your life to ministry of any nature, then you have experienced distractions. Mind numbing, never ending, ever increasing, absolutely frustrating distraction. If you have not, do not worry they are on the way. I promise you the enemy pulls out all the stops, and uses every opportunity and person to effect distractions never dreamed of to keep you from your appointed task. The only defense I found was to remain resolutely focused on task, depending upon the Lord to clear the way. I know that sounds very trite and much easier to say then do, it is and it is, however, it is the only way.

Immediately and most obvious in our case, making a living and paying the bills, became a major distraction. It was apparent very soon that my continued association with Gerald and the business was one of *those* mistakes. Not only did they, Gerald and the business, require a great deal of time, but there also were no funds forth coming in the way of salary, and most certainly not for the ministry. Upon the selling of my stock, tithing on behalf of the business had ceased immediately. Tithing was pronounced to be unaffordable, I was unable to convince the partners that tithing was not a question of affordability, but a necessity. Almost over night I began to see the results of that decision as bid after bid was lost and projects began to go amiss, eating deeply into their budget and profits.

A brief aside; it is said in scripture and I paraphrase, that if we do not praise Him, that the very rocks will cry out and praise Him. Giving freely from that which is given is one form of praise, and experience has taught me that if you are greedy and refuse to give, blessings slowly cease and you wind up in worse condition that you were in the beginning. I know there are a lot of theological studies, teachings and doctrines in disagreement to what I have just said, and my only counter to them is my one personal witness and experience.

To continue.

I had started a spinoff project manufacturing a product for Gerald and his associates to sell. During the first couple of months this seemed to work well. The project generated a good income providing salaries for four employees, while keeping Debbie and I afloat and the bills paid.

Gerald began to demand more of the sales total for his side of the ledger. He was extremely jealous of our apparent success and extremely greedy. He refused to accept that our giving had any thing to do with our small success, insisting that our manufacturing cost and portion of the product sales was therefore to high.

We were constantly negotiating the cost of the finished product, its pricing and the percentage which would go to the sales side of the ledger. Finally I told him the cost of manufacturing was as low as it could possibly go and if he did not like it he could by product somewhere else, as it was I barley covered manufacturing costs. Gerald kept on with his demands and even tried to hold payment from us. The only alternative was to sever the relationship. This I did, leaving us once again without income, and our only prospect for covering our needs, the Lord. Funny how that works out!

I mention finances first in an effort to dispense with them. Finance was to be an invariable problem, a condition which I am certain was not and is not unique to us. Over the next few years we suffered greatly due to the lack of finances, yet because of them we were able to partake first hand of the wonders and miracles of the Lord, as he gave them from His hand.

My participation in Bible School became impossible and I withdrew in early April, just a few short weeks from graduation. I could no longer afford the time the classes required. My constant attention was required at the shop to keep things going. Debbie was also required at the shop to help, when she was not in school. We were being swallowed by our efforts to provide a living for ourselves and fund the ministry through business. All the while everything got steadily worse, we seemed helpless as we watched everything erode away. What I did not know then, but know now, is that God had a plan and resources different than mine.

One day in late March, much to my surprise, I realized that in all our hard work and all our business, work on the vessel had not progressed. In fact nothing had been done at all since the beginning in late February. Our hard work and efforts while good intentioned and seemingly focused on the project, had been for the most part distractions keeping us from the intended work and goals. I had constantly sought the Lord for answers to our financial woes, but He had been silent.

Suddenly I awakened realizing that, at least in part, the reason for our being here had been ignored. Sure intentions had been the best, but I had not been told to build "Stepping Stones" for Gerald to sell. I had been commanded to build a ship. I did not know if this was the reason for the silence, however, I now realized I must above all else build the vessel as the Lord had commanded. At that moment a resolve was planted within me which I could not shake, nor could any around me lessen that resolve. Over the next years many tried and more than a few times I cried out to be relieved, but the resolve never weakened, and whenever I asked for guidance or cried out for relief, the answer always came back, **"Build My boat and preach My word, preach My word and build my boat."** I began to work on the boat.

I called a meeting and told everyone, I asked for and expected their cooperation, as our only reason for existence as a company and their pay checks was the construction of the vessel S/V Maranatha. I issued instructions to Lewis, (Debbie's friend) to act as foreman, a big mistake, over the manufacturing process. I would be present as the boat building took up one side of the building and the manufacturing the other. I would spend my time working on the boat an offer assistance to the manufacturing process only when needed. I was still in overall charge, but Lewis would be responsible to see to it that the orders were completed.

The two other young men who worked for us full time were brothers and Christians, they readily agreed and were excited, offering to help with the boat whenever I might need help. Lewis was strangely quite. We ended the meeting on a positive note not felt among us in some time, and I spent the remainder of the day and early evening completing the lofting floor.

I believe the single most destructive force within a ministry is lack of submission. I know as Christina believers we have all submitted to the Lord, or at least we are supposed to have submitted. What I mean here is submission to the ministry to which you are called to serve an uphold. I do not desire to paint a picture of abject submission to tyranny and drudgery or any of those negative connotations. I know a statement like this brings to mind, especially to the free wheeling independent, me myself alone American mind, pictures of becoming a mindless robot to the master. Not the submission I have reference to here.

Without exception every Christian, mostly Evangelical Christians I must admit, has something they refer to as "my ministry," the other types of Christians, main line denominational folks, I have met mostly do not have, nor look for anything even remotely resembling "my ministry." When queried most respond with a statement something in this order,"that is what we pay the preacher for."

When pressed to define ministry, those who profess to have a "my ministry," usually offer some vague description, such as ministry to young people, old people, etc. Rarely do they seem to have any detail and most always retreat to, "I'm just waiting on God/the Lord and His timing." I submit that for 90% of those folks, this is no more than an excuse to do nothing. Possibly worst of all are those who join another ministry under the guise of support and submission to its principles and goals, all the while using that ministries facilities and resources to promote their own agenda.

This may not sound important, however, remember "a house divided cannot stand." The result of "Christians" such as these is fractious, since they are constantly at odds with the ministry, since their goals and purposes do not in mesh. As I have stated prior to this a call to minister to homeless children is not the same as a call to unwed mothers. If a person who has a call to unwed mothers enters a ministry to homeless children and does not put their call aside during their tenure, the results will be fractious and non-prosperous. They are at cross purposes even though they are serving the Lord.

Another more positive scenario might go like this, a ministry to homeless children by definition probably also serves homeless mothers with a portion of those being of the unwed verity. A person with a call to the unwed mothers could join to serve that community, however the over all call of the ministry would be to homeless children, not unwed mothers. Even when all involved are very careful and dedicated to the primary ministry call, the meshing of personalities is difficult. When they are not, it can be disastrous.

Submission, I speak of here, is of your talents and services submitted to the purpose and call of the mission to which you have attached yourself. The most destructive thing in an individual church body is a person who is not committed to the call of that body, but to their own agenda. This is the single most reason for "church hopping" in contemporary church bodies.

Such was the case with Lewis. I had always had some misgivings regarding him, yet, he was my wife's friend, and she considered him to be a brother. When plans to begin the ministry and move to our new location had taken shape, Lewis had asked to be included. He stated he believed in what we were doing and wished to be apart of it if possible. He, like the rest of us, needed to make a living, but his salary requirements were not excessive, so I welcomed him into the ministry. I made it clear that the first priority was the mission God had given us, and that all else was to be of little consequence. He agreed and was a great help making the move.

A few days after the meeting in March we learned of the real reason for his industry. "I think we need to talk," Lewis said as he entered my office. "I'm not sure I like what you had to say the other day. I've got a lot invested in this business operation and I don't think its right for all the proceeds to be spent on your ministry. I've got my own ministry and I was looking forward to using proceeds from this business to fund that also. I just don't think you can do what you said."

I was taken by surprise, needless to say shocked. "I don't believe I understand what you are talking about," I said. "This entire operation is owned lock, stock, and barrel, by Spirit Wind Ministries. It is a nonprofit corporation, there are no owners except God. We have a board of directors, because it is required by law, but no one has any stock in the business, that's the way a nonprofit corporation works. No one has any interest in any of this, it is all owned by Spirit Wind ministries. We are all just employees and that includes you. Proceeds from any enterprise we are engaged in are dedicated to the construction of the boat and the furtherance of its ministry and nothing else. What you do with your salary is your business, but as far as having any claim on any of the ministry funds or materials you don't. You need to understand that right now."

"You mean I don't ever have any chance of owning any part of this outfit," he asked?

"That's right," I answered, "I don't know where you ever got the idea, but if you recall I made that very clear when you asked to come with us. You said you understood, but wanted to be a part off what we are doing."

"Well this ain't my ministry and I need money for that," he stated, "I think I should have half the business because I'm doing all the work while you play with the boat."

"Well Lewis, that's not going to happen," I countered, "First of all because the business belongs to the ministry and second I see no reason why you should be given half the business just because you think your doing all the work. You are an employee, and up till now, a valued one and a friend. You're being paid to work here, right now there are no funds for a raise, so don't even ask. You have a claim on nothing other than your salary. If you wish to continue in your present capacity you are welcome and needed, but there is nothing else. The funds of this organization will only be used to further its goals and programs, not yours or those of anyone else."

"Well if that's all I get," he stated, "I guess I'll stay. I need my pay check, but I still think its a hell of a way to treat a fellow Christian!"

He returned to work, but I must admit it was a mistake to allow him to stay. After a few days things seemed to return to normal and he appeared to be the same old Lewis. Yet, I did spend more time in the manufacturing area solving problems and helping to get out orders. Spirit Wind Ministries had developed its own version of "blue flu."

During the next months the relationship with Lewis remained cordial, yet, there was always a reservation on his part, as if he was just waiting and watching, for what I did not know. We would to our amazement, find out what he was watching and waiting for, one Sunday in June. Just before our next move, Lewis unlocked the shop, while no one else was there, loaded half of all the tools, forms, and epoxy resin onto his truck and drove off without a word to anyone. Our brother in Christ had committed grand larceny!! But I am ahead of the story.

TOOLS AND MONEY,
MONEY AND TOOLS

As the weeks passed, life settled into a predictable routine, even a normal life. The boat construction, though slow, was progressing. The bills were being paid, however, we never seemed to have more than $79.00 in the bank. Money was a constant headache.

Shortly before we opened the building Pastor Rodger introduced me to Tom. Tom was the head usher at church and had been a fisherman in California. Pastor thought Tom would be of help to us, so he brought us together. Tom among other things was a cabinet maker and worked in the Oklahoma City area as a finish carpenter and cabinet maker. During the course of our conversation he offered to furnish his tools for the construction of the vessel, as long as he could use them also for his business. I accepted the offer gladly as we had no tools and believed we could work out the details of joint use. In short, I could see no conflict with this arrangement.

As soon as the lofting floor was completed in late March, Tom moved in his tools and set up shop. He really set up shop! There were a large number of tools, and he also required a large area to warehouse his materials and supplies. He also needed a large work space and of course all was without rent or utilities as we were to use his tools. Will I never learn?

Even though we had 8000 sq, ft, of space, by the time we met his requirements, we were somewhat crowded. I began to get the feeling the construction of "Maranatha" was expected to take second seat to Tom's cabinet shop. I was troubled by all of this, but decided to go along with him, as we needed the tools. He was, after all, a brother in the Lord, so he must be sent to us by God, so how could it go wrong? Brother, oh brother, did I still have a lot to learn.

The Lord had placed us next door to a young man who had just began a hardwood lumber business. After much searching for lumber suppliers, I decided to use our neighbor as our lumber supplier, he seemed honest and his prices were defiantly competitive. The only draw back, if it were one, was that he only ordered in bulk and there was always some delay in getting the material.

We finally settled on Honduras Mahogany and ordered 8000 board feet in random width and length of one inch minimum thickness. The price was $1.61 per board ft delivered to our door, this was at the time an incredible price, even though I had no idea as to the quality of the materials ordered. I had the right of refusal, and more importantly, I had given the whole matter over to the Lord. I expected Him to see to it that we were supplied with the material we required.

Even at this incredible price the bill for the lumber was still to be well over $12,000 dollars, which is no small sum. We did have on the books enough orders to fund the transaction and the funds would be collected by the time the lumber was to arrive in four weeks time, some where around the 15th of April. I had made a large deposit upon making the order, which once again left us with a remaining balance of $79.00 dollars in the infamous bank account. While we waited for the lumber to arrive the lofting lines were completed and made fair. By the first week in April all was in readiness, waiting for the mahogany to arrive.

A large row of columns ran down the middle of the building supporting the ridge of the building thirty feet above the floor. In order to have enough room for the construction of the vessel, the lofting floor was raised vertical and secured against this row of columns, effectively creating a wall dividing the building. This was accomplished one afternoon with the help of the manufacturing staff and everyone else we could grab to help.

Once this titanic effort was accomplished, with the help of strong backs and several cable come-a-longs, there before us was the "S/V Maranatha" as she would be some day. The full size drawing of the hull as it was to be constructed was simply huge. None of us had really comprehended the true scale of the vessel we had undertaken to construct. While lying flat on the ground, the lines had not conveyed the same proportions as they now did standing vertically before us. There was a real feeling of excitement as we stood there, even Lewis seemed impressed.

During the next weeks as we waited for the lumber to arrive, I began construction of a dinghy which we named "Honey." I also was required to keep up a running battle with both Tom and Lewis, to keep either or both, from taking over the space required to construct the S/V Maranatha. What no one except Debbie, understood or wanted to understand, was that the "Maranatha" was the only reason we had the building in the first place.

I was on the brink of learning a very valuable lesson about the greed and envy possible of our brothers. I continued to try and find where I was at fault, for surely I must be in error, I must be the one who needed to change. Surely there was fault in the positions I had taken. Echos of those voices of years past while I was in the hospital returned to haunt me. I bought into the enemy's lie, for I knew only too well from whence I had come. I knew how weak and lacking in faith I was, I began to listen to the others, tried to do as they said I should do, not what God had said to do. I did not recognize the trap then as I do now, after all these people were my brothers in Christ, so how or why would they lead me wrong?

As I listened to those around me I took my eyes off Jesus. That is the mistake common in the Christian world, not unique thankfully to me, but common enough to be recognized and dealt with expeditiously. I listened to the religious around me, and forgot to listen to the only one who truly knows what He is doing, and slowly things around me began to deteriorate.

There were some bright spots, however, the Mahogany arrived late one afternoon. It was in a closed van so we could not immediately see the material. I gathered everyone to help unload, as the driver backed the truck into place, and began to break the seals to unlock the doors of the truck. As the doors of the truck opened we saw stacks of dark red boards almost completely filling the truck. I jumped into the truck as I was very anxious to inspect our lumber. I reached out and touched the first stack and was instantly knocked down by the power of the Holy Spirit and became drunk in the Spirit and was consumed with a strong urge to laugh. The driver jumped up to see what was wrong and was also slain in the Spirit. I began to pray and give thanks for the safe delivery of the lumber, as I did the power lessened and we were able to touch the wood and begin unloading. The driver turned out to be a brother in the Lord, and as we unloaded, all of us became happy in the Spirit, as we handled the lumber. We sang and gave praises of thanksgiving to the Lord.

Our neighbor who owned the lumber company, had fallen away from an active Christian life, and at the time was separated from his family. Yet as he helped with the unloading, he too was affected and came under conviction. He was to tell me a few days later, that he had, as a result of his experience that afternoon, made a new commitment to the Lord and returned to his family.

"Build My boat......"

As the days and weeks passed I was to see many changes in the people who had reason to handle the lumber. Some, however, could not touch it or get close to it.

The lumber itself varied in length from 8ft. To 18ft., and in width from 12in. to the widest being an incredible 36in. wide. Thickness ranged between 1 ¼ in. to 1 ¾ in. All rough cut. Our excitement increased as we unloaded the broads for we noticed there were no broken boards, no knots, or blemishes of any kind. In short the material for the skeleton of the "S/V Maranatha," her ribs, beams, and keel was perfect.

Over the next weeks and months there were those who for want ever purpose attempted to steal or otherwise appropriate some of this blessed lumber. On several of these occasions I witnessed as they were physically repelled, as if electrically shocked. I witnessed them turn, run away and never return. On one occasion I watched as five men, first attempted to steal the material, and when foiled in that effort, attempted too set the lumber on fire, only to once more be foiled by the power protecting the stack of wood.

Tom and Lewis both became agitated by the presence of the wood. Tom could not approach closer than three or four feet to the material. I thought this strange as I knew he loved the Lord with all his heart. Yet, he was repelled because, I believe he was not the one who was to work with the material. As work progressed on the various parts of the boat I realized I was the only one who could work with the wood until it had been sized, shaped and placed into its proper location in the hull.

Tom began to lock up his tools. This effectively prevented me from working unless he was present, and then only if he did not need them. Finally one day in May I told him we had to come to some agreement, for I could not continue to support his private business if the tools could not be used for the ministry, as was our original agreement. I was informed he was moving out anyway, since he had decided the ministry and the boat project were not of God, and he could no longer be part of it. I was shocked! I simply did not know how to react to a statement like that.

I asked him why he thought the ministry and boat were not of God and he said, "If you were truly of God you wouldn't be having money problems. God just doesn't work that way."

"Is our church and Pastor Roger of God?" I asked.

"Of course it is," he said.

"Well, why then is the church having money problems?" I asked.

"That's different," he stated in a rather frenetic manner as he turned away. He spent the rest of the day and the next moving his tools and supplies. Leaving with his last load he stopped to say goodbye and his last indignant words were, "I just can't stay with something that's not of God." As he departed I heard ghostly voices from my days in the hospital uttering similar condemnations.

Here I was again, accused of not being "of God," mostly because I was resolute in following the vision as I had been shown. But, all of the old accusations flooded back. I knew how inadequate to the task I was, I was and am not a towering intellect, I do not posses inordinate skills, nor am I in possession of mountains of wonder working faith. As a representative of God's Kingdom I am woefully inadequate. I simply love the Lord with all that I am, that is all I have to recommend me.

For some reason known only to His unfathomable mind He chose me for this project and to that and that alone am I responsible. This was not the first time I had heard words such as these from self appointed gatekeepers of the Kingdom and it would not be the last. Yet, God in His infinite wisdom had chosen me, so therefore, even with and possibly because of all the difficulties, and my own doubtful nature, I must and would go on.

Needless to say work on the boat ceased for a time. Two dilemmas required solution before we could move on. First I needed to check myself out with the Lord. I had no doubts about "being of God," but I sure needed to find out were I had gone wrong, if indeed I had. Where had I missed it?

Secondly, I had to figure out how to build the boat without tools. My first dilemma was not so easy to answer, I was already surrounded by detractors from all sides, and Tom's departure only added fuel to the fire. Since, as I stated above, I always considered myself unimportant and totally inadequate for my calling, I had a natural tendency to accept part if not all of the concerns others voiced about how the ministry was conducted.

Search as I may, however, I found nothing in my actions toward Tom to justify his actions or charges. The second dilemma was quite easy to rectify, for the time being at least. I earnestly sought the Lord for a solution to the problem and once again the answer came back, to look around and do with what I had been given. The Lord is nothing if not consistent!

This I did, and found I could accomplish the construction of the keel with the tools I owned. A circular saw, drill motor and bits, square, hammer, screw drivers, and a right angle grinder. So the work resumed once more in earnest and the great 400 pound back bone of the S/V Maranatha gradually took shape.

About this time the manufacturing orders began to fall off and efforts to switch to another product line failed, due as always to a lack of money. I reluctantly closed down that part of the operation and let everyone go including Lewis. Lewis was not happy about this, he informed me that he still considered himself to be a partner if not the owner of the business. He made some threats about taking what belonged to him. This I did not take seriously since nothing in the place belonged to him.

I doubled my efforts to raise funds in the fashion everyone told me ministries raised funds. I began contacting other ministries in the area asking for help. With the help of Pastor Roger, Debbie and I had joined a pastors conference in the area, so I started with them. We received lots of encouragement, but no funds. When final payments began to come in for the last orders delivered, I realized unless we received a miracle in funding we could no longer pay the rent and utilities, let alone continue to build.

I was on the verge of a great mistake, as hind sight tells me. I sometimes marvel at how dense I remain.

Efforts to raise money through other ministries met with little success, however, a few meetings did produce some interesting results, life long friends, and near disaster.

One evening after presenting the ministry to a small congregation, a young man introduced himself. He told me he was the director of operations for a large commercial construction firm in Oklahoma City. He ask about the method and plans for transporting the S/V Maranatha to the nearest waterway large enough to allow passage to the Gulf of Mexico. After some discussion he said he would discuss the matter with the owners of his company, but he was reasonably certain they would donate use of their heavy equipment to make the move when the time came. I invited him to the shop to see what we were doing first hand. I was presented with an offering from the congregation for which I was truly thankful. I departed and frankly did not think about Jim and his offer as my mind was occupied with other things.

Scriptures tell us that our Lord has enjoined us to not worry, "take no care for tomorrow," and all that, yet we do it anyway. We spend the majority of our time in worry about one thing or another. How imperfect and inattentive we are! If we could only learn to listen as He has taught and equipped us to do.

The following afternoon to my pleasure and surprise Jim and the leader of the congregation walked in the door. They were the first people to show enough interest to come and check us out. They were warmly welcomed and given the nickel tour.

Jim was appalled at my lack of tools, being in the construction business, but was none the less impressed with what was being accomplished with the tools at hand. Both were greatly affected by the "wall" as it had become known, and the full size of the vessel depicted on its surface. The most exciting thing, however, was the news Jim brought from his employers, Lippert Brothers Construction Company.

That morning had been the time of their regularly scheduled board meeting and Jim had presented our ministry and our need to them that morning. He told me they had been very impressed as he had told them of the audacity of our vision to build such a vessel in the middle of Oklahoma. After some discussion they had passed a resolution to make themselves the official transportation company to Spirit Wind Ministries.

They would furnish whatever equipment and manpower required to transport the S/V Maranatha whenever and as often as required. I was overwhelmed, I could hardly believe it was true. More importantly, and much needed for Debbie and I, it was a sign from the Lord. There were people out there in the most unexpected places, who loved the Lord, who could catch the vision and join with us in our efforts. Many prayers of thanksgiving were voiced, and Debbie and I had light hearts for a change.

Little did we realize the true value of this pledge, yet, as time passed and as the pledge ran to fulfillment we stood in awe of Lippert Brothers Construction Company and their dedication to us and to their pledge to the Lord.

This association was also our first experience with those Christians who belonged to other than our own charismatic evangelical circles. The owners and most of the board of this company were main line Lutheran, their families had been Lutheran for many generations. Coming as we did from our "free wheeling Spirit filled" background, we were at a loss to understand their acceptance of us. We had been placed upon a path of learning. We found, that despite what we had been taught, labels and doctrines invented and developed by man do not and cannot restrict the God we serve and love. All Christians, Spirit filled Christians, are not housed only within the confines of the Pentecostal Charismatic doctrines and their congregations.

You just cannot put our God in a box. He simply does not fit. He's too big!!!

A few days later I found myself talking to a man who had been asked to contact us by the leader of the congregation where I had met Jim. I soon discovered him to be a very wealthy man who had made an enormous fortune from his invention and manufacture of a very well known piece of medical equipment. He made it a practice to donate the majority of his income, millions per year, to ministry, especially mission programs. I was very excited and when I told Debbie, she hardly could believe what I was telling her. Over the course of the next several days we had many conversations discussing the vision, our plans, everything he could think to ask about us, and most we discussed in some length.

Finally one day he asked, "Do you believe in speaking in other tongues?"

"Yes," I answered.

"Have you ever done it?" he asked.

Yes I have," I said, "I have my own prayer language in which at times I pray in the Spirit and on one or two occasions I have been used by the Spirit to bring forth a message at the appropriate moment during service and at times bring an interpretation as is required by scripture."

"Well I don't believe in all that," he stated, "I believe tongues are given as required to communicate the gospel to the lost. By that I mean, if you are sent to a Spanish speaking region as a missionary, the Lord will have you speak Spanish or what ever language is required to convey the message of salvation."

"I don't have a problem with that," I answered, "I know of several cases through my studies where just such a thing happened. I know if the need arises I will be given the language required for the situation and so will anyone else under similar conditions. However, that does not do away with the personal experience I've had with my prayer language or the messages in tongues I've been witness to in service. I have been present at times when it was obvious someone had gotten carried away, but that does not negate the scripture or make all messages in tongues inaccurate. The Holy Spirit seems to have a way of letting those in authority know what is legitimate and what is not. I put my faith in Him and the leaders of the body to which I have submitted to tell the difference. Also, anytime I have been present during one of these times, the Spirit within me has always witnessed to the truth or error of the event."

"I have determined over the past several days," he began, "that you and your call to ministry are legitimate. However, I think this boat thing and a ministry involving seagoing vessels is ridiculous. I just don't see how it can work, and quite frankly I think it is a waste of time. I tell you what I will do. If you will give up on this crazy boat idea, I will fund your ministry for whatever it takes. I will fund you to anywhere in the world for as long as you wish to remain in the field. I will fully fund all your personal and ministry expenses for as long as you require. I will set up a trust fund in your ministry name to insure the funds are always there. You can use the funds in anyway you see fit with the exception of anything to do with boats owned and operated by the ministry. I don't agree with that, I believe you are sincere in you belief in the visions and all that, but I am not convinced. Well what do you think?"

This time the silence was all on my side. I did not know what to think, I was stunned. "I'll have to talk to my wife and we'll have to pray about it." I finally answered, always a good escape.

"Take your time," he said, "the offer is permanent, so take all the time you need."

I had heard of this kind of thing happening, but I never dreamed of it happening to me. I do not remember what Debbie and I talked about as we discussed this amazing offer, but I am sure we tried hard to find a way to accept. Wouldn't you? To be set up for years to come, to do ministry unencumbered by financial worries. I know many who would love to have been in our shoes at that moment. There was, however, one very large condition. In truth I knew my answer before I ever hung up the phone.

Even though the offer was terrific, to put it mildly, if I gave up the building of Maranatha and all she represented, I would be going against my call. Somehow I knew if I were to submit to these conditions, no matter where we went or what ministry work we involved ourselves in, it would not prosper. It would make little difference how well funded we were, or how well intentioned our efforts, it would not be the ministry I was given as my call through the visions. I would not be "building His boat nor preaching His word" as I had been instructed.

A few days later I called the gentleman and told him exactly that, I thanked him for his generous offer and I never heard from him again.

By this time it was mid June 1985. The back bone of S/V Maranatha was ready for assembly it consisted of four pieces. The stem, the ballast keel, deadwood and horn. The bank account had a balance of $79.00 dollars and so I come to another part of the story.

PART III

THE JOURNEY TO COMPLETION AND LAUNCH

ALL HELP IS NOT SENT BY GOD!
OR
THE CREW

In June of 1985 two events happened almost simultaneously. We obtained our crew and we met Brother Ray and Brother James of the Grace Rescue House.

The first members of "the crew" were Greg and Jessie from Grand Isle, Nebraska. I met Greg and Jessie during a trip to visit Debbie's mother over the Memorial Day weekend. We had been invited, by an old friend of Debbie's, to meet with who we thought would be a potential backers. Instead when we arrived we discovered the group consisted of Debbie's friend and Greg and Jessie.

I made the presentation and then spent several hours answering questions, mostly from Greg. During our return trip Debbie told me she thought Greg would ask for he and Jessie to join the ministry as crew members. I had some reservations, mostly because it was very early in the schedule of things, and I had not yet heard anything much from the Lord about crew. Possibly because I had not as yet asked. We needed the help, so with Debbie's help, we developed a plan for bringing aboard crew for the S/V Maranatha.

Another young man named George and a young woman named Lois joined us shortly after our return from Nebraska. They were both homeless young people who had settled at the Grace Rescue House. We met them there and after meeting them several times, in that setting, they asked if they could join us as crew members.

All four arrived approximately at the same time, so Debbie and I set about arranging our new household of six.

The new members of the ministry would be put to work building the vessel, working in the office, and helping to raise funds. We decided to move to a larger apartment, hopefully at a lesser rent, and as far as practical live together just as we would on the vessel. Financially the ministry would supply room and board as well as personal maintenance items. The plan was also to eventually supply clothing and an allowance. The ministry would not and could not accept responsibility for personal debt. One of the conditions for acceptance as crew would be assurance that any outstanding obligations were settled for at least the term of enlistment.

All of this may at first sound slightly utopian, but one must consider that once underway the six people serving aboard the vessel would be living and working in exactly those same conditions. The ministry would be directly responsible for their well being through the Captain of the vessel. The majority of operations would take place in international settings and waters, therefore, international maritime rules would apply.

I have never believed a volunteer should have to pay a ministry for the privilege of volunteering. I realize this to be the accepted practice of most ministries today, but that does not make it correct. I do believe it is wrong for a person to join expecting the ministry to assume financial burdens other than those required for the physical support of the ministry and its personnel while on the mission field. This support would necessarily include those left behind maintaining the ministry and the mission crews while working at the home port.

I am talking here about personal debts such as credit cards, car payments, mortgages, and so on. I believe, and I believe the scriptures back me up, that a ministry is responsible in loo of salary to supply all the personal needs of its people, while they are enlisted with that ministry. Further I also believe they are responsible to assist in re-establishment once a missionary returns to life outside that ministry.

I realize there are an enormous volumes of questions and details to be addressed in a program such as this, such as length of service and so on into infinity. No one standard would apply to all missions or situations. The scripture does tell us that "the workman is worthy of his hire." Some how I think we have managed to change that verse to read something like, "the workman has found us worthy so he must hire us."

I am not including the mini-missions, those where people rush in for a few days, a week or two at most, of feel good because I am doing good, only to rush home to declare the magnificence of a successful mission. These mini-missions in my opinion, create a great burden on the long term missions in the area and most assuredly should pay their own way. I know, why don't I say how I really feel.

Missions would be better served if the money spent on "quickie" missions were gathered together, and used to establish a more long term work, or to support one already in place. This belief was foundational for our discussions and formulation of our plan of operation concerning crew members.

Pastor Roger as president of the Bible School had given full scholarships to any and all staff of Spirit Wind Ministries who I wised to enroll. This I felt would be invaluable, for even thought I would never dream of telling any who joined us what or how to believe, I knew that if we all graduated from the same Bible School, we would all be operating from the same background.

Over the course of several long telephone conversations during the month of June, all this and more was discussed and agreed to by Greg and Jessie in Nebraska, and the others at the Grace Rescue House. I still had an uneasy feeling, but Debbie was excited about her friends joining us and we did need the help. All were accepted as crew conditional upon a ninety day get acquainted period. It was determined they would join us in mid July, giving them time to settle their affairs in Nebraska.

The stage was set, and by the time of their arrival Debbie and I had relocated to a large three bedroom apartment on the south side of the city, centrally located to the shop and school. All was in readiness, both Debbie and I believed we had done all we could to prepare for this next phase of our lives and the ministry. I still to this day believe we had, yet, our biggest problem remained finances and we were constantly calling upon all of our faith to keep that area under control.

We anxiously awaited the arrival of our crew. Debbie and I both were looking forward to the support and companionship crew members represented. I have not yet mentioned the isolation we had began to feel, even though surrounded by people. There seemed to be few who understood us, or our mission, as we did. We believed with the addition of crew, who would be immersed in the work as deeply as we, there would be four more people who would understand. Our hope, or one hope at least, was that there would be four more like minded people standing with us, adding the kind of support that comes only from those with like experience.

Two days before Greg and Jessie arrived the other momentous event occurred. We were asked to speak at the Grace Rescue House. The invitation came through a friend who had been on their board for years and who also served on our board. The Grace Rescue House was, most people thought, an outreach of the church community. It was not as we found out, but was founded by two men who at the time were homeless themselves. They were allowed to "camp" in an abandoned commercial building on the south side of the South Canadian river, if they would act as watchmen to protect the building. Over the years they were there, they began to allow other homeless persons to "crash" there for short periods. Eventually others began to give them support funds, food and so on and the Grace Rescue House was born. However, there was never any formal church or denominational association.

We accepted the invitation as an opportunity to present the Gospel to the lost, an assumption most evangelicals, especially those living in the Bible belt make, to them everyone not like them is lost. We had a lot to learn.

Our friend went with us one afternoon to meet the two men who administered the Grace Rescue House prior to our speaking there, at their request. They were introduced to us as Brother Ray and Brother James, and for that reason we like everyone else in in the city assumed they were Catholic Brothers, or at least had been at one time. After a short visit, the time and date for us to speak was set and we departed as they were extremely busy. A few days later I called to confirm the schedule, again at their request, and was told the program had changed. They wished us only to speak about our mission and goals and nothing else. I thought it strange, because I knew with the type of work they were doing the people who would make up the audience would most likely not be able to participate in helping our work. None the less Debbie and I arrived as scheduled. We had been invited to dine with them prior to the meeting, so we arrived around six in the evening.

The dinner was an experience in itself. We discovered all those present were, about thirty people, were staff persons and permanent residents of the Grace Rescue House. All had one way or another found their way off the streets to the Grace Rescue House and over time had come to work for the Brothers in various ways. These people were the ones who carried out the day to day operations at the direction of the two men.

Grace Rescue House at the time was located in an old two story building where temporary and semi permanent living accommodations were provided. A daily feeding schedule was operated from the kitchen and lunch room facility serving three or four hundred meals twice daily. A food pantry type distribution, to those in need, also took place twice monthly.

Recently they had added a large abandoned church property which they had occupied on a temporary basis pending negotiations for its purchase or donation. This property was close by the school location and contained a very large kitchen, gymnasium, numerous classrooms, and offices. The classrooms and offices had been converted into quarters for the staff, for as we were to learn there existed a very strict class structure among those who lived within the influence of the Grace Rescue House and the two Brothers. It was to this location we went to have dinner and make our presentation.

As you might imagine there were many varied and spellbinding stories among the people we met that evening. Stories of addiction, crime, and poverty, even stories of adventure. There were stories of deliverance also, but as I look back one fact stands out clearly. Despite the name Grace Rescue House there were only one or two who even mentioned The name of the giver of Grace or gave Him credit for their deliverance, and then gave it very quietly. At the time I did not pay too much attention to this as I was sure the Brothers were devout followers of Our Lord and Savior Jesus Christ. I was to learn, as time passed in this association, that there is more than one Jesus in the world, but I get ahead of my story.

I made my presentation, which was warmly received. Afterward Debbie and I spent several hours answering questions and visiting with the very interesting people we had met that evening.

We felt relaxed and revived by the enjoyable evening. The hour became late and we made our goodbyes. As we thanked the Brothers for our meal and their hospitality, Brother James presented us with a check, stating he wished it could be more. I was surprised as I had not anticipated nor expected a donation from this meeting. I slipped it into my pocket, unopened as was my habit, and replied saying the any amount was more than enough and surly blessed by God.

We departed making our way home in silence. Each thinking of our evening and the people we had met, thanking God for places like that, who were reaching out to the dross of our society, providing food and shelter as they struggle to survive. I looked at the check after arriving home and was shocked to see it made out in the amount of five hundred and eighty seven dollars. I was speechless as I handed it to Debbie, we could not believe our eyes. Never had anyone given us this much money. It was enough to pay our rent and utilities, all due, with enough left over for groceries. We rejoiced greatly that night.

Over the next several days Debbie and I decided to offer our assistance during our spare time, mostly evenings, to the Grace Rescue House. We had been given an open invitation to visit, so Debbie and I returned to make our offer to assist in their ministry. The offer was graciously received and thus began the single biggest mistake I was to make. An error in judgment which over the next several months would, but for the protection of the Lord, almost see the end of the ministry, the vessel, and our own personal lives. Strong words but fact none the less.

Greg and Jessie arrived a day or two later and the next several days were busy ones, getting them moved in and settled, introduced to the shop, acquainted with the work and introduced to friends and supporters.

One problem quickly reared its head, as upon arrival Greg informed me he had just bought a new pickup truck. Despite all the discussion prior to their being accepted, he stated since it would be of use in the day to day operations of his part of the ministry, he expected the ministry to make the payments for him. He was flatly told there were no funds available for that sort of thing, as he had been informed prior to being accepted, and his coming to Oklahoma. The ministry was simply not going to meet this personal obligation. He was told he would be allowed time for a part time job to earn the funds required, but he would be expected to meet his obligations to the ministry. I must admit I was livid as I once again explained all of this, as I had weeks prior, during his acceptance interviews.

He finally decide I meant business, and we continued under slightly modified conditions. I should have terminated our association then and there, but I did not. As it turned out the truck featured prominently in his departure several weeks later. Greg, Jessie, Debbie and I became very active at the Grace Rescue House and developed a work and ministry among the street people, who were always of great number and need. The two other members of our crew were met during our visits.

George, and Lois were both from broken homes and homeless. They had been working on staff at Grace Rescue House for some months and were highly recommended as ones I should chose to fill out our crew. I was reluctant, they were both pleasant enough, but due to living conditions I felt they should be the same sex or another married couple. I also felt the need for caution in selection as the Bible School was a nine month commitment, representing tuition loss to the school for each of our crew members. I wanted to make sure the crew was correct, as there were five such scholarships involved, amounting to a great deal of financial commitment by a small struggling congregation and school on our behalf.

Debbie, Greg, and Jessie applied all the pressure they could. I was to find out later Greg had made promises in the name of the ministry he had no way or authority to cause to happen. Finally I relented, George was to remain in residence at Grace Rescue House. This was agreed to by the Brothers, and Lois was to move in with us. George was to spend his days and evenings in and with the rest of the crew. His residence required a juggling of schedules to transport him to and from as he had no personal means of transportation. At mid-august the five were enrolled in Bible school and despite my initial reservations, all appeared to be going well, at least on the surface.

In an effort to weld us into a cohesive unit several steps were taken. Sunday morning service was attended as a group at our church or the church where we were presenting the mission and ministry was mandatory. As it turned out we never made a presentation during the Grace Rescue House months.

One hour each evening was set aside for group study, prayer, and discussion, attendance again was mandatory. These meetings never lasted only one hour and during the course of the first months were a source of much camaraderie and learning. It seems, however, all this was very much too good to be true.

We began to have a total drought of funds, almost immediately upon our decision to associate ourselves with the Grace Rescue House. I spoke with several pastors I knew from the pastor's association and discovered the Grace Rescue House was almost totally ignored by the church community in the city. Any associations that did occur never seemed to last more than a few weeks, always ending in permanent and complete severance of all ties on behalf of the departing church or ministry.

I in my naivety could not understand this as the work was certainly worthy. I never got a definitive or straight answer, even from our own pastor or those who were closest to us. God, that someone would have told us the truth. Instead they held firmly to the old tradition of never speaking ill about your brother.

We are so stupid sometimes, knowing something is not right but allowing others to enter into danger without ever speaking up in caution. The only person who did even hint that all was not right at the Grace Rescue House, was our friend, the one who had introduced us to them in the first place. However, he did not come right out and warn us about further association, he just sort of disappeared into the back ground.

By the time Greg and Jessie arrived from Nebraska, it was evident that our time at our building was coming to an end. There simply was no money to pay the rent and the bills. If something, a miracle, did not happen quickly everything was going to end. The donation from the Grace Rescue House was, I thought, a God send. I took it to be a sign from the Lord, but I was to learn not all help comes from the Lord, and He does not bless that which He has not sent, regardless of the source. Sometimes, more often than we realize, help is sent or arranged by our enemy, for the purpose of gaining a foot hold from which to work the destruction of the Lord's work.

Only Debbie and I were fully aware of the gravity of our situation, and when Greg and Jessie arrived we felt it only right to share this information with them since they were joining their lives to that of Spirit Wind Ministries. Debbie and I were not overly concerned, for we had seen the Lord work his miracles before, usually at the last moment.

Greg, however, apparently had had no such experience and consequently during a conversation with the two Brothers, he informed them of our situation, in I am afraid somewhat embellished detail. The Brothers offered a possible solution which he accepted without consulting Debbie or me first. The result being an offer which caused me to make the almost fatal mistake mentioned earlier. I assumed it had come from God, after all the offer met all of our personal need and almost certainly insured the success of our project and mission.

The Grace Rescue House had recently accepted the gift of an old church camp near Dale Oklahoma, about twenty miles east of the City. Their plan, as presented to us, was to establish a residential community for those "street people" who wished to and had the ability to leave the street. There were several large dormitory buildings, three residential houses, a kitchen and dining hall, a counselors residence building, which was to be set aside for our use. In exchange for acting as ministers to the people who would live on the property, and for acting as camp managers, they would provide the following; Space for the construction of the S/V Maranatha, the residence building, and food and utilities for us and our crew during our tenure. All the buildings were greatly run down and required much repair before they could be occupied. Therefore, they would pay our rent where we currently lived while we worked to ready the property for occupation on a permanent basis. They would also begin immediately to supply us with food provisions, thereby freeing our limited funds for use in other areas of need.

It was determined after a quick trip to the "farm," as it became known, that we could begin to move all the materials, supplies and everything associated with the boat to the property immediately. Work would stop on the vessel for a while, but as this offer of salvation surely came from God, this was deemed acceptable.

I then made the gravest mistake of the ministry, I accepted the offer! Arrangements were made and by the first of August we had vacated the shop building, moving all the equipment, supplies, and assembled structures of the vessel to the "Farm" at Dale, Oklahoma. Our friends from Lippert Bros. Construction providing the equipment to make the move.

THE FARM

August 1985 was a very busy month for the members of Spirit Wind Ministries. The crew, Debbie, Greg, Jessie, George, and Lois, were busy during the morning hours with Bible School. I kept busy in the mornings working for a printer. No salary was involved, but in exchange for my help he printed our news letter, cards, and any other printing needs we might require.

Afternoons and Saturdays were spent repairing our headquarters building at the Farm in anticipation of our moving in by September first. Sundays, except for church, were free days and were spent in whatever form of relaxation was deemed appropriate by each individual, at least that was the plan. Usually, Debbie and I wound up playing house parents, with it seemed increasing frequency.

Around the middle of the month we received a utility deposit refund in the amount of three hundred eighty five dollars. Greg immediately claimed it as coming from God to meet his first payment on his pickup truck as it was the exact amount of the payment. I reminded him of our many conversations on the subject of paying for his truck. I also reminded him he had made no effort to secure part time employment to meet his obligation. He was upset by my attitude and remained convinced the ministry was to pay for his truck.

Greg, was not a bad person, rather he was the type of Christian who belongs to a group of believers I have named the "Happy Holy Club." I am sure you know someone of this type.

Greg's idea of ministry and Christian life was living with constant chill bumps. All he really ever wanted to do was stand around, or sit as the case may be, deeply engrossed in discussions of theological philosophy. Hopefully maintaining a high degree of Holy Ghost chill bumps.

Each day without end, he was constantly searching for some topic which would bring all other activity to a halt, and provide him with his required chill bump fix. All exterior distractions which prevented this from happening, were deemed by him, to not be of God. Therefore, unworthy of his time or consideration, up to and including work or paying his bills.

As I have said he was not a bad person, just naive and useless. He as you might imagine was not a very happy individual most of the time. He was especially disturbed to discover the word ministry means work, and most of the time very hard work. Also disturbing, was the discovery that the chill bump supply derived from our morning and evening worship sessions, was meant to last him through the day. Everyone was busy working in our various ministry duties and could not stop to enjoy a lengthy discussion in order to develop Greg a fresh chill bump fix. He was a chill bump junkie!

Jessie was a delight and very stable in her faith and her own self. Secure in her relationship with the Lord. She worked hard and was doing very well in Bible School. She seemed to enjoy all we were involved in doing, nevertheless, she began to show the strain of the constant mothering required by her husband, in order for him to remain in his immaturity.

Greg and I spent many long evenings during July and August, talking into the very late hours of the night, discussing his feelings and how he could adapt them to the reality of mission work and daily Christian living. Sadly, each time we had one of our discussions, we always covered the same territory. Greg seemed forever mired in the "Happy Holy Club." As my grandfather used to say, "He was so heavenly minded, he was no earthly good."

A few days after the refund incident Greg informed Debbie and I they would not be going with us when we moved to the "farm." He and

Jessie were to take up residence at the Grace Rescue House and were leaving Spirit Wind Ministries. The reason given was, "we just did not fill their needs." In other words, I would not pay his truck payment. None the less, it was a sad day for us, we had both grown to love them very deeply and even as exasperating as Greg was at times, I believed given enough time, he would make an excellent member of our team.

Greg did, even though leaving the ministry, wish to continue Bible School on the scholarship furnished because of his being a member of Spirit Wind Ministries. After prayer and discussion with Pastor Roger, it was agreed to let them continue, as we felt it would be most beneficial for Greg to complete the course. However, within two weeks time Greg's welcome at the Grace Rescue House House ended, for reasons I have never learned, and they returned to Nebraska. Except for a very brief visit to retrieve some personal belongings, Debbie and I have not seen them since.

George and Lois helped us move to the "farm" headquarters in early September. Both young people seemed to be flourishing. Lois was a good companion for Debbie and George, though reserved, always seemed to have something of value to contribute to our efforts. Within days of our moving to the farm we began to have troubles, minor at first, but there seemed to be a constant running battle with the Grace Rescue House.

First, the amount of time I spent working on the vessel verses working on repairing the buildings, to allow more people to move to the farm was an issue. Secondly, our nightly bible study and the results coming from it, became an issue.

The first issue was temporarily resolved by my agreeing to cease work on the vessel until all the buildings were repaired. This was a temporary solution, for I soon discovered that not only was I to do the work, I was also expected to supply the materials. I was informed that since I had all that lumber, the mahogany, stacked up out there I was to use that for the repairs. After all I was told the people needed the repairs accomplished in order to have shelter for the winter. I flatly refused.

All work stopped on the buildings except for plumbing and there was a lot of that to do, since over the years every pipe on the property had frozen and burst. What seemed strange though, as the days and weeks went by, was that it was only me who did any of the work. By this time there were thirty five individuals living at the Farm other than our crew. With the exception of the Spirit Wind Ministries building, living conditions were little more than camping out, less than one step from the streets.

The men spent their days standing around with their hands in their pockets, and as the weather grew colder, they built fires and stood around them chewing tobacco and swapping tales. All effort to enlist them in anything resembling work met with the strongest of opposition. Gradually everything ground to a halt.

George returned to the main complex in the city and dropped out of Bible School. He worked in the kitchen and after some investigation I found he had tried to leave on several occasions, but could not cope with life outside the Grace Rescue House. It seemed he required the rigid structure and security imposed by the two men who rule over the Grace Rescue House. Lois remained with us. She prospered and was a great help and companion to Debbie.

During our time of renovation prior to moving to the Farm, the Brothers had moved another couple to the Farm as co- ministers with us. Together Larry and Janie, Debbie and I were to share the responsibility of keeping order and seeing that everyone was fed. The meal schedule alternated between their house, Larry and Janie, and ours. Yet it seemed regardless of the schedule, we were always feeding at least ten or twelve extra for dinner in the evenings.

Since Debbie and Lois were in school everyone was on their own for lunch and breakfast. Weekends always presented us with twenty to twenty five to feed twice daily, no small task since our only stove was an apartment size electric range. We had no refrigerator, only a large upright freezer. We were kept well supplied with food stuffs, so in that regard we managed quite well. The first indication we had of real trouble came in the form of an edict, from the Brothers to stop conducting our nightly bible study sessions.

You will remember these were started as an effort to bring our crew closer together, as well as a time to be with the Lord in study and worship. Shortly after our moving to the Farm, Larry and Janie asked if they could be a part of the study sessions. They were welcomed warmly and soon after others of the residents asked if they could also join. In a very short time almost all who resided on the farm gathered nightly in our home to worship, praise and study the word. Many great blessings came as a result. Larry and I were excited as we could see a slow, but never the less, change taking place among the people.

Two weeks prior to the edict the Brothers moved another couple to the Farm as resident ministers for the dorm buildings. We welcomed them as the four of us could use all the help we could get. The resident total of "street people" was now fifty plus and all of them were in great need in one fashion or another of ministry.

This new couple, however, immediately ordered all the residents to have nothing to do with either Larry and Janie or Debbie and I. When this was brought to the attention of the patriarchs of the Grace Rescue House, it was denied and the four of us were made out to be the heavy's in the matter. Things moved rapidly from that point. We were ordered to cease our worship sessions and all residents were told if they associated with us in anyway they would not be allowed to eat. We continued our worship and study sessions and all who wished to attend were welcome.

We began to seek the Lord for answers and a place to move to, as we were sure this was only going to grow worse. Next came a threat to cut off our utilities if we did not stop preaching and teaching freedom in Jesus. We were ordered once again to cease all worship sessions, other than those conducted by the last couple moved to the Farm, and another couple who brought the number of resident ministry couples to four.

We continued, and the Lord remained silent, but there were a series of warnings which came through Debbie. The Lord began telling her in advance, the next move they were going to make, and what we should do. This was for several weeks simply to stand firm. The utilities were not cut off for that would have required the removal of service to the entire complex. They did, however, cut off our food supply.

Strangely during all of this turmoil we were never asked to move, the only thing required was our complete and utter submission to the two patriarchs of the Grace Rescue House. It was during this time that we made the discovery, that no one at the Grace Rescue House was allowed to read the scriptures on their own. Bible Study was allowed only under the guidance of the two Brothers, and only their interpretations were allowed to be discussed.

We definitely preached a different Jesus from the perversion we discovered was taught at the Grace Rescue House. The lives of all who resided at the Grace Rescue House were subject to absolute control in virtually every aspect of their lives.

The method of control we quickly learned was supply or denial of food, cigarettes, coffee, and the most prized of all Pepsi. Only those who wished to get off the streets were subjected to this control. All others who came were fed twice daily, given a place to sleep, if available and otherwise ignored. This was the underlying reason for the establishment of the farm community. It was an effort which would enable the removal of those subjected to this form of subjection, from the immediate view of the public and supporters in the city.

By the middle of October our nightly sessions had shrunk to Debbie, Lois and myself. Larry and Janie came occasionally, but since threats had been made against them also, they were uncomfortable leaving their house and children unattended. We would alternate holding our worship and study sessions between our houses. One evening as Debbie and I returned to our dwelling, after attending one such session at their house, the Lord gave Debbie the first of many warnings.

"The death angle is among you this night, seeking who he may destroy. Protect yourselves, anoint your door posts."

When Debbie told me this, I quite frankly did not know what to do, but I had lived closely with the Lord for sometime by then so I knew something must be done. We returned to Larry and Janie's, only a few yards away and told them of the message. We gathered in prayer and felt impressed with a physical urgency to anoint all exterior openings as soon as possible. This we began to do, friends were staying with Larry and Janie, so there were seven of us and it went quickly.

As Janie was descending from the second floor, she suddenly fell down the stairs, from about two thirds of the distance from the floor. She came to an abrupt halt at the bottom of the staircase and immediately declared she was unhurt as we rush to help her. When the excitement died down, she told us, someone or something had pushed her as she started down the staircase. She had felt two very cold hands, in the middle of her back, and had been pushed very hard. As she fell toward the floor, she felt like two very strong people, one on either side, caught her and guided her to a soft landing at the bottom of the stairs. She said as she reached bottom she felt herself being placed very gently to rest. She was convinced she had been rescued by the Lord's angles. I have no doubt in the truth of that fact either.

We all rejoiced in her safety and quickly departed to warn all the others and anoint the dwellings. All accepted the warning that evening except at the dwelling of the overseers sent by the Brothers. I myself knocked on their door and was informed they would receive nothing from anyone out side their official group and I was to leave immediately. This I did and was glad to do.

Debbie and I returned, with Lois, to our home. As we did we could feel a presence about us, not the Lord, but something else very dark and sinister. We were not afraid, due to our warning, and the precautions we had taken. We stood outside our door for a few minutes. We could not see anything, but we could detect something moving about the grounds, from building to building.

It was a still night with no breeze, yet the trees were moving as if the night itself was causing them to shake. We went inside and remained in prayer until after midnight, when just as suddenly as it appeared, the feeling of dread disappeared and peace returned.

The next morning we were awakened by a loud pounding at our door. An elderly woman who lived in the house where our warning had been rejected, wanted to use our phone, we had the only telephone, to call the authorities. When asked why, we were told that the nine month old baby of a couple staying in that house had died in the night. Debbie and I looked at each other in wonder and of course all assistance offered by us or Larry and Janie was rejected.

We learned a few days later, that when I had knocked on their door that fateful night, I had interrupted a seance. All those in residence were required to attend, failure to do so would mean immediate eviction from the farm and return to the streets. The man appointed by the Brothers, his name was Marshall, also announced the he had been given total authority and his instructions were law. No one was to speak to or even acknowledge the presence of anyone on the property who called themselves Christian. Needless to say we were shaken and sought the Lord for a means of escape from that place.

Surprisingly we still had a number of people to feed daily. These were the ones who were, despite their street lives or possibly because of their street lives, strong enough to stand and resist the pressures being put on them to conform to the Grace Rescue House dictates. These poor folks found themselves out of favor and food, so they came to us and we fed them as they came, asking no questions. We simply gave thanks that we were able in a small way to help them.

On one occasion I witnessed Marshall pick up a club, and approach a young man named Paul, cursing him and making all manner of vile threats to his well being. Paul had been one who had shown promise at the worship sessions and had shown interest in the Farm at the beginning. As Marshall approached him, he stood straight and firm. He raised his arm, pointing straight at Marshall's chest and said in a loud clear voice, "get away from me you foul laying devil!" Marshall recoiled as if struck in the chest by lightning, dropped his club, turned and ran away foaming at the mouth, babbling unintelligible words.

The next morning Paul came and asked if I would drive him into town. He had been evicted from his room in the middle of the night. It seems that the reason for his troubles the day before was that Marshall thought his quarters were too good for him. Marshall wanted him to move to another less comfortable place since he was resisting and not conforming. He had spent the remainder of the night in the woods, not wanting to disturb us till morning. We fixed him some breakfast, got him warmed up, gave him what little money we had on hand and took him to town and we never saw him again.

That morning while Paul was eating his breakfast he told us some of his story. He told us he was a fugitive from the law. He had been convicted of burglary in Illinois and had jumped bail prior to sentencing.

He told us that he had decided to return and turn himself in and serve his time. He had decided to do this he said because of what he had learned during his time with us in our worship sessions and by watching us as we confronted life on the farm.

He had, one night several weeks prior gone into the woods, knelt and gave himself to the Lord. He said that during the confrontation with Marshall the day before he was frightened, and did not know what to do, when suddenly the words he spoke seemed to just come out of his mouth and he was saved.

He told us that when they came for him in the night, ten or so men came to get him, but they could not for some reason touch him, they just surrounded him and forced him out of the room after he had gathered all that belonged to him. He believed this to be conformation of his decision to return to Illinois and serve his punishment for his crime.

He knew he was protected and that he would be safe, for he was in the care of God. I think of Paul often and for me he is is proof that even in the midst of hell on earth the Holy Spirit is working the mighty miracles of God.

Debbie and I were in constant search to find someway out, but the Lord was silent. We told no one of the happenings on the Farm as it seemed everything we did say fell on deaf ears. We trusted no one except the Lord and he continued to warn Debbie about events to come.

One morning He told Debbie they were going to try to destroy the Maranatha. All that existed at that time was the keel, with the stern frame and seven mold frames standing in place, but not yet fastened to the keel as there was no money for bolts.

We agreed in prayer when she told me of the warning she had received. I left the house going to the top of the hill where Maranatha rested. I never got to the top of the hill. I was stopped about one hundred feet from the top by something and stood rooted to the spot. I watched in horror, and then in wonder, as I saw Marshall leading a group of men toward the back bone of the vessel.

They were carrying axes and sledge hammers, their intent was obvious. As they came to within about fifty feet or so to the structure they were stopped as if they had run into a brick wall. They circled around the vessels skeleton baying and howling like a pack of dogs, yet, they never got closer than fifty feet to the objects they sought to destroy. Finally, after what seemed an eternity, they returned to the side of one of the buildings where they stood looking at the Maranatha's structure and me, cursing loudly. Even though they stood cursing me and the vessel with all they could muster, they did so with a very bewildered look on their faces.

I then went up the hill to begin work for the day, for I knew they could not stop the work. My work surface which contained the lines for the construction of rib frames was about twenty feet from the structure and as I began preparations to lay down another rib I was startled by an angry scream. I looked up to see Marshall running straight at me with his ax raised. I did not have time to react, I stood there and watched as he was knocked flat on his back by an unseen force.

As this was happening another group of men carrying gasoline and a torch headed for the stack of mahogany in an attempt to set the lot on fire. This failed also, for as they doused the material and applied their torch, the gasoline simply would not light and they were driven out of the shelter where the lumber was stored slapping at their heads as if they were being attacked by wasps or bees. The next morning when I returned to work everything was as it should be and there was no odor of gasoline about the mahogany.

I wish I could say I stood firm and preached the Gospel to Marshall and to those who witnessed the event, as he lay there on the ground, but I did not. I gathered up my tools and returned to the house. We were never again bothered by Marshall and when we finally departed the Farm he seemed genuinely sorry to see us go. We never talked after that incident, but something had changed in him.

Larry and Janie departed the Farm around Christmas time. They were badly shaken and their ministry, as well as their personal lives, had pretty much been destroyed by the attacks they had endured, while we were standing our ground on the opposite side of the compound. Neither of them ever went into much detail, but I know if half the rumors were true, they faced as many deadly and vindictive attacks as we. Their armor, however, was not as strong for whatever reason as ours. Larry gave up ministry and they divorced shortly after leaving the Farm.

During all of these events and our tenure on the farm, there were some bright spots believe it or not. Paul's confession on the morning of his departure for one, and Lois. Despite all efforts from the patriarchal throne in the city, she was still with us and had bloomed into a whole person. She had been freed from the street embittered young women who had joined us in August. We also at times saw around us the touch of the Lord's hand on the people who had come to live at the farm, and once in awhile we were able to witness as, like Lois, one broke free of the bondage of the street into the freedom of the Lord.

Mostly, however, it was a day to day pitched battle. We watched as emissaries from town would arrive on their appointed missions of destruction. They were always intent upon destroying our work and the lives of those who refused to submit. Even Marshall, after his failure and change on that morning of confrontation, found himself being pushed out of leadership to be replaced by yet another head ministry couple. Delegations of five or six would arrive in the middle of the night and with "Gestapo" like tactics pack up dissenters and take them away, they hoped, never to be seen again.

One couple did appear one morning asking if they could have something to eat and gather their thoughts on what to do next. They had two children both grade school age and needed to think. We discovered they had relatives in Arizona whom we contacted, and they sent money for bus tickets, so we were able to send them on their way we hoped into safety.

Most we would never see again. I suppose this was not unusual since they came from the streets. Yet, I will always wonder what happened to them and where they went. There were a few inquiries, since some were picked up by law enforcement, and they complained of their treatment while at the Farm. On one or two occasions I was able to tell a local sheriff's deputy of some of the things I had witnessed, but other than the farm becoming closely watched, to my knowledge no action was ever taken.

BEN

We met Ben a few days after moving onto the farm. He was our neighbor living just a short distance on down the road. Ben was an instructor at the county Vo-Tec school, he also was a part time deputy sheriff. Upon learning of our projects he offered the loan of his tools if we would move them to the farm. We were over joyed and accepted immediately. We soon discovered Ben's tools filled two very large trailers and it took us two full days to move them. He also included box after box of supplies, nails and screws. A very large blessing. Ben became a regular visitor to the farm and on occasion we would take several of the residents with us and visit Ben's church on Sunday for worship.

In late November Ben mentioned he wanted to use one of his saws for a honey-do project. He was told he had to get permission from Marshall to enter the building where his tools were housed. I might mention here, that I had quit using Ben tools by this time, because the hassle was just not worth the energy it took.

When he pursued the matter he was informed by Marshall that he was no longer welcome on the property and he needed to move his tools or they would be sold for money to pay the electric bill. It is a gross understatement to say he was extremely upset.

Larry and I took him to our house for coffee, to warm up and cool down. As we explained what had been taking place over the last few weeks he not only had difficulty believing what we were telling him, but when he realized we meant what we were saying, he was appalled.

Ben then found Marshall and flatly refused to move his tools, telling him that he had given their use to build the boat and would not take them from me. He further stated he was a part time Deputy Sheriff and if one item was sold or came up missing he would see to it that everyone involved would spend a great deal of time in court and possibly in jail, especially Marshall.

One thing that got the residents attention was any possibility of confrontation with the law, for many and sundry reasons.

The reaction from the throne room in the city was to cut the power to the shop building by physically cutting the power line to the building. An attempt was also made to set fire to the shop and the stored mahogany. This attempt was foiled as were all the others by the protection the Lord had placed around us.

Shortly before Christmas Ben came to Debbie and I and told us he had told our story to his father in law who owned an acreage south of Luther, Oklahoma. His father in law had offered to let us move to his property. We could live in a rather old and dilapidated trailer house parked on the property. I told him I was overwhelmed by the offer especially since his father in law did not know us. This would allow us to escape from the farm, but I told him, we had no money to pay rent. Ben told us that none would be needed, his father in law kept a horse on the property and if we would take care of it for him and watch the place for him, that would be our rent. We would be expected to pay our own utilities, it was not much he said but, "the price is right."

The next day we journeyed to Luther about thirty or so miles distant to inspect the offered place of refuge. It was dismal!

A barren wind swept hilltop with no out buildings, except for a makeshift lean-to, as a wind break for the horse. A small prefab tool shed serving as feed storage and a very old one bedroom trailer house. The trailer house on closer inspection had at one time been used as a chicken house and currently was being used to store tools. There were holes in the floor, no running water to the kitchen and the bath room fixtures were missing. I was assured that the plumbing and bathroom would be repaired, and though it was afar cry from what most people would be content to call home, it could be cleaned and made livable.

Like Ben had so aptly observed, "the price was right." As dismal and as rundown as it was at that moment, the place would release us from the persecution we currently suffered, and there was a peaceful presence about the place.

Debbie and I did not accept the offer right away, however, perhaps we had grown gun shy, but for whatever reason we delayed. After much discussion and increasing pressure from the throne room in the city, we accepted the offer and began preparations to move.

Strangely up to this point our moving from the farm had not been the issue constantly pressed on us by the patriarchs in the city. The issue was our refusal the cease our independent worship and our refusal to submit to their dictates to cease teaching the truth and freedom of the grace we have been given in Christ Jesus our Lord. This we had steadfastly refused to do, yet, when we announced we were moving, a series of strange events began to take place.

Various people, mostly overseers sent to control the population, began to take actions designed to placate us. Strong efforts were made to convince us to stay. When these failed stronger actions were used, these were designed to force us to remain on the property. Our old car was tampered with, in an effort to deprive us of transportation, this failed due to a warning to Debbie.

I was informed we would not be allowed to remove any of our furnishings from the house since we could not prove they belonged to us, we did, and that attempt failed also. And attempt was made to take physical possession of the boat and materials, claiming it all belonged to the Grace Rescue House. This was easily beaten back by producing invoices which would prove if needed, that everything associated with the boat project belonged to us.

Finally Ben's tools were placed under lock and a constant guard by those in charge. Thanks to Ben's longtime residence in the area and his association with the Sheriff's office this maneuver was also beaten back. I am convinced with certainty that Ben was sent to us by the Lord. Though angered he helped us face each challenge with a cool head, which those attacking us could not match. Without his help I am not sure we would have escaped intact. They were trying to work their mischief on his turf and in Ben, with God's help, they met their match.

Finally, a day or two before Christmas, the Lord told Debbie to beware for they were going to try to move into our home and physically take over to prevent our moving. Debbie told me of this last warning and I wondered, all our arrangements were made, we were to move on the third of January, surely now they would leave us alone. Yet, because we had learned from experience to depend upon Debbie's warnings, we prayed, accepted it with thanksgiving.

Scarcely an hour later there was a knock on the door, "they're here," Debbie said. I answered the door and was brushed aside as fifteen people rushed through the door quickly taking up stations throughout the building. They were attempting to pick up our possessions, but they were prevented by the same force that had thwarted every other attempt on our property or person. The more they persisted, the more they became frustrated, distracted, and very agitated.

The leaders informed us that they were moving in and that we were to furnish them with full access to the entire facilities and use of all furnishings. One of them asked for the phone since they needed to call the throne room. My words. They wished to inform the Brothers of their success in taking possession and preventing us from moving. I informed them all, that when they began paying the phone bill they could use the phone and not until then.

With this I was informed I was acting in a belligerent and non Christian like fashion. I also told them to leave the building immediately. I reminded them that, they knew we were moving on January third, and after that they were welcome to the place. Until then it was our home and they were not welcome.

They became very belligerent and began making threats towards us personally and towards our possessions. After all the times they had tried and been prevented they should have learned by now. Unknown to me or anyone else, the Lord had told Debbie to call the Sheriff. While they were distracted and making their threats, she had done just that. Our persecutors had posted a guard outside our door and as they saw the deputies entering the drive, warning was given, and they all exited as quickly as they had entered. There was spirited conversation outside our home as those not afraid to do so confronted the deputies. In side, all was peaceful, as the Spirit of the Lord filled the place.

Shortly the deputies entered and I described what had taken place. They were fully aware of the conditions and situation through their association with Ben. We were assured they would keep an eye on things until we could leave. They advised us that our safest course at the moment was to leave if at all possible. I told the deputy I was aware of that, but we had property to protect, Ben's tools among them for instance, and if we were to leave without them, all our possessions would most certainly be destroyed. As he departed, he stated rather matter of factually, "better your property than yourselves."

I was greatly disturbed and asked Debbie if she wanted to leave right then, but she told me, "the Lord has protected us so far, and he will see us through the move and beyond." So we stayed.

On January third, Lippert brothers Construction once more came to our rescue with their trucks and equipment, loading the Maranatha and the balance of our equipment. In the midst of jeers and curses, we turned our backs on the Grace Rescue House, the Farm and all that went with it. Shaking the dust off our feet as proscribed in scripture.

SHORT RIBS OR MANNA

Since miracles are an integral part of this story, I thought I would pause at this point to tell you of just one we experienced, while on the farm.

In previous chapters I mentioned that when we began our association with the Grace Rescue House our incoming funds began to cease. By the middle of October our total income was reduced to twenty five dollars a month, which came to us regular as clock work, from Debbie's mother. Until the writing of this story she was never told of our condition, she was just contributing to the ministry as she had from the beginning. As a matter of fact we told no one of our financial straits, as we knew the quickest way to failure was to admit to our fellow Christians, that we were experiencing very difficult problems.

No one wants to hear anything but good reports from visiting ministries. People, it seems, only believe you are blessed of God if you always have a glowing report to give. Admission of difficulty is a "negative confession" and is a sure way to not receive another invitation and a small offering at best.

We, Debbie and I, had faith in the Lord. To be sure we did not at times understand what He was up to, but we had faith. We used the twenty five dollars to best advantage, mostly gas for the car. Debbie and Lois made the trip to school each day, and if there was not enough gas or money, we would pass on going to church occasionally. No one was the wiser as we from time to time visited other churches and we were not missed by our home church on these occasions. Our food supplies were cut off by the patriarchs in the middle part of October.

We had a goodly supply on hand, so we were not concerned for the moment. We continued to feed all who presented themselves at our door and as you might expect the food supply dwindled quickly. About this time, I do not remember when or from whom, we were given two ten pound boxes of beef short ribs and a one hundred pound sack of potatoes.

The days went by, Debbie and Lois went to school. I tried, unknown to them, to find employment and was unsuccessful. Each time I would cry out to the Lord, I got the answer that had frustrated me off and on for years.

"Build My boat and preach My word, Preach my word and build My boat."

I must admit as I watched our meager food stocks consumed by as many as twenty people per meal, I grew more and more concerned. The vegetable supply ran out quickly, and most mealtimes, lunch or dinner consisted of short ribs, potatoes, and prunes. We did have a goodly supply of oat meal, flour, corn meal, and powdered milk. We also had this enormous box of prunes! I did most of the cooking, since Debbie and Lois did not get in from school until late in the afternoon, so I invented many ways to prepare ribs, potatoes and prunes.

We also from time to time, would receive gifts of canned goods from the pastors of our once a month meeting. They knew we were feeding many people almost daily and contributed to that effort, but knew nothing of our dire financial straits. The first box of ribs went quickly and the potatoes dwindled. The prune box seemed bottomless and we quickly grew tired of prune cake, prune stew, or prune whatever. Finally no one would eat them but me, and by then, I just cut them off the pit and mixed them with my oatmeal in the mornings.

The coffee ran out and there was no money to replace it. I have been and am a confirmed coffee drinker since childhood, so this was a great blow to me. For a time we had tea, but that disappeared eventually and only water was served with our meals. Yet, we still had ribs, potatoes, and prunes. The second box of ribs was half gone and the sack of potatoes was now half full, still we had potatoes and ribs every meal. Sometimes it was just Debbie and I and at other times it would be ourselves and fifteen or so people who lived on the Farm who sat at our table and were served a meal. The large meals occurred mostly on weekends when for some reason the "overseers" were absent, basking at the throne of the patriarchs, while receiving new instructions for the coming week.

Surprisingly I never thought much about our supply of ribs and potatoes, I just gathered what was needed for the upcoming meal, and never thought about the remaining quantities. One day in mid November Debbie commented that we should be running out soon, then it dawned of me that we had been preparing meals from these items for close to a month and using a goodly quantity each day.

I went to determine the remaining quantities expecting to find the larder to be empty. I discovered we still had one half box of ribs and one half sack of potatoes, and that we still had a goodly supply of powdered milk, corn meal, and flour also remaining.

Our only meat was the ribs and we used them as required each day, lunch and dinner without thought to how many were being used to meet the need of the day. Every evening we had ribs and potatoes and infrequently some type of canned vegetable, which for some reason always seemed to be some form of canned corn or stewed tomatoes. More and more frequently, our meals consisted of ribs, potatoes, gravy, and corn bread. By the end of November that was our steady diet. Oatmeal for breakfast with ribs and potatoes for lunch and dinner, yet we still had one half box of ribs and one half sack of potatoes. In December the guests for each meal dwindled until it was only Debbie, Lois, and I to feed each day. We managed quite well and stayed healthy and did not lose much weight, but I would have killed for a nice green salad.

We had used from each item daily, for the preparation of each meal, in the quantities required to prepare for the number to be fed, without thought for the amount remaining. Yet, when we moved from the Farm on January 3rd, 1986 there still remained one half box of ribs, one half sack of potatoes, one bag of oatmeal, one bag of flour, one box of powdered milk, one bag of corn meal, and ten pounds of prunes to be moved with us.

After moving to our new place in Luther, Oklahoma, we continued to eat our meals from these provisions. They were all we had to eat. Shortly after our arrival in Luther, we began to once again received financial contributions and Debbie got a part time job with Circle K stores.

As the money increased we began once again to purchase food supplies, much as normal people would. I, as did my wonderful wife, enjoyed the first fresh vegetables and salads we had eaten for what seemed like years, but was only months. I felt like Ben Gunn, a character in Robinson Crusoe, who when rescued from the island could only ask for cheese.

One afternoon in the middle of January 1986, I went to the freezer to get our ribs for dinner and to my surprise the remaining one half box of ribs had spoiled. They were unusable. I also discovered the remaining one half sack of potatoes were rotten, not one could be used. Of the remaining supplies the powdered milk was gone, the flour and corn meal were full of weevils and the prunes, bless them, were covered with a thick green mold. In short, all were spoiled for use, just since our evening meal the day before.

I was at a loss for a moment, for we had depended upon these food stuffs for our survival since the middle of October past, some three months. No matter when or how many to be fed, they were always there, and there was always the same remaining as when we had gathered from them to prepare the coming meal. Now suddenly they were gone. My first thought, I am ashamed to admit, was what are we to do now. Always the worry wort I am, I am.

Debbie was due home and was expecting a meal. How could I explain the loss of our food to her? She had stood beside me and suffered with me during these long months, how could I now explain this? I turned and returned to the house, and discovered a pantry and refrigerator full of fresh supplies, purchased with our new found funds. I welcomed my long suffering and wonderful wife home that evening with a meal of vegetable stew, pasta and chicken. Not ribs, potatoes, and prunes!

We rejoiced greatly for our spoiled manna, and we humbly thanked the Lord for His provision of the beef ribs, potatoes, and prunes in our hour of need. He had provided as He has promised to do. During our long walk through the valley of the shadow of death He walked with us, and as He has also promised, He never left us nor forsook us.

I to this day cannot face a plate of beef short ribs! I am, however, ever mindful of our Lord's provision which Debbie and I still enjoy.

LUTHER

. . . .

Our new residence sat on a red Oklahoma hill top some five or six miles southeast of the small town of Luther, Oklahoma. We were most definitely in the middle of the country, fifteen miles southeast of Edmond, Oklahoma and some twenty miles northeast of Oklahoma City. As I stated before only minimal buildings existed on Jason's farm, the father in law's name, including the very old ex-chicken- tool house, trailer house which was our home.

The first days were consumed in rejuvenating our living quarters, and efforts to protect the tools and supplies from the elements. Our plumbing problems were only partially solved, with the bath room being repaired to a state where we had both hot and cold running water. The missing commode had been replaced and the bath shower was serviceable as long as a bucket was placed under the valve while running water. There was no water to the kitchen and regardless of the amount of time materials and effort expended in that direction that short coming was never solved. The entire time we lived in the chicken house trailer water for kitchen use was drawn from the bath room in the winter and from a garden hose in the summer.

Holes in the floor were covered and with a very vigorous cleaning by Debbie, the last traces of the chickens and tools were vanquished, at least as long as we occupied the place. We once more, thanks to Debbie, and thanks to her genius for such things, we soon had a snug and very pleasant home.

Lois, much to our disappointment shortly prior to our move, announced she would not be going with us. She felt things were moving too slow for us, and quite frankly she had lost confidence in our project. I cannot say I blamed her, considering all we had gone through, she also was under constant barrage from her past associates at the Grace Rescue House to dump us and return to them. This, to her credit she did not do. She made arrangements with Pastor Roger to stay in a loft apartment within the church building.

She continued to attend Bible School and church and she graduated with Debbie in May of that year.

After graduation she established herself with an apartment in the city and a job. When we left Luther for the water a year later, she was doing well on her own, and was no longer a street person. Some good did come from our time at the Grace Rescue House!

The outside surrounding the house was another story. The S/V Maranatha's back bone sat in the open approximately fifty feet behind the trailer. Another fifty feet or so beyond that were piles of supplies and tools covered with plastic and tarps. The makeshift feed shed was crammed to the brim with tools and miscellaneous stuff Jason had removed from the trailer. A two horse trailer was also packed tightly with tools and supplies, there was no other shelter.

Before anything could be done the weather interceded with a heavy snow, which covered everything, and did not melt away for several weeks. I spent this time helping Debbie and trying to find work or some way of funding our work and our living.

Deb and I for the first time in months found ourselves alone, by ourselves with no one around us, alone. There were no close friends who came to visit and the associations we had through the church and pastors association were insulated due to distance and our lack of funds. Many of our friends had moved and we had lost touch with them and they with us. Virtually all our worldly ties and possessions had been striped from us. It seemed all that which remained was Debbie and I alone to finish the work.

The unfinished skeleton of the S/V Maranatha and the corresponding stacks of beautiful mahogany lumber sat there covered with snow accusingly, waiting for us to complete the work we had started almost one year earlier in February 1985, with so much joy, hope and determined faith. Had it really only been a year?

———∞∞◦❖◦∞∞———

During the month of January and early February 1986, while we waited for the weather to clear, Debbie and I would journey into Oklahoma City. She went to Bible School, and I went to a little church in the northeast part of town. The pastor had a project, the result of a vision, and she thought my drafting and design talents would be useful in developing this vision into a visual document or documents.

I sat up a drafting office within the offices of the church and each morning I would go with Debbie to work on this project. With hind sight, I believe the purpose for this activity was for cleansing and restoration, on my part. I accomplished little on the project, for try as she might, Pastor Renee could not convey her vision to my mind and hands, it simply was not my vision. However, during those days I spent there, I was cleansed of the residues which had attached themselves to my attitudes and thoughts during the warfare on the Farm.

Renee, the pastor, was a prayer warrior and each morning was given over to prayer first, for as long as it took, for a release to come. Nothing interrupted the morning prayer until the call was released. Hence, Debbie arrived from school many days out of the four we came to town, just as the prayer was ending or finished. So little to no work was done on the project, but a lot of work was done on my spirit and soul. I spent many hours in the prayer room and as the days went by my spirit lightened, and I once more felt the desire to build, and just as importantly the certainty of completion.

Debbie had been impressed to work for Pastor Renee cleaning her house as an offering to her and was staying after school two days a week to work in the house. I reduced my trips to town to those two days and I once more began my efforts to build.

The first project tackled was an attempt to put the tools and work space under some sort of shelter. We had a great deal of standard construction materials that would not be used in the construction of the vessel. The remains of the lofting floor for instance. A rather large shop building was started with that material. The size and layout of the building was the result of a three way conversation between myself, Ben, and Jason. These three way conversations were really two way conversations with either Ben or Jason being absent and conveying the thoughts of the absent party second hand. Therefore, surprise, surprise, confusion raised its head and certain parts of the details needing to be conveyed were very often found to have gone missing.

Jason thought I was going to supply all the materials, and I thought Jason was supplying the foundation and floor. I was to supply the remainder from the construction materials I had on hand. Jason and I finally got together and discovered that most of the plans for the building existed only within Ben's vivid imagination. Neither Jason or I possessed the funds to construct a shop as envisioned by Ben, consequently the building was never properly finished. The design was modified to form a temporary tent like structure which was adequate for the term of our stay. Even though the structure was severely damaged by one of Oklahoma's notorious storms, it served as a shop, even though roofless, for the balance of our stay on the hilltop east of the Oklahoma town of Luther.

All during my attempting to help Pastor Renee and get our dwelling and grounds organized, I had constantly sought the Lord for direction and guidance. We needed income, if for no other reason than our own existence. Our move had resulted in no rent, yet, we were responsible for the utilities and our own food. The only answer I got was one I had heard so many times it is etched in my soul even now. **"Build My boat and preach My word, preach My word and build My boat."** I at times, would stand there alone on that red wind blown hilltop and scream with frustration. Had I not done all I could to carry out those instructions? Had I not in the process of doing this brought my wife and I into penury, even to the peril of our very lives? What more could

I do? I had given all I had, we had nothing left, no funds and no help. Essentially as I stood there and looked upon the place where we lived, we were penniless and homeless with a partially completed vessel and a pile of lumber hung around our necks like the proverbial millstone.

WE BEGIN ONCE AGAIN

One morning in mid February, the month of Adar once more, my wonderful wife and I sat at breakfast discussing just this conundrum.

"It seems as if for whatever reason, nothing is going to work for me unless I'm building that stupid boat!" I stated rather forcefully. "Everything is blocked and all I get from the Lord is build my boat. Doesn't he know we are in need of many things to do this?"

"Well," she said, "seems to me if that is what He wants, that's what you'd better do!"

I hate it when she is right! Nothing else could be said to that.

I went outside to consider the task in front of me. The snow was gone, it was a mild sunny day, and rare for Oklahoma there was no wind. I realized as I stood there pondering my problem, there was nothing to prevent me from beginning to build once more, except myself.

The problem before me was this, the mold frames constructed prior to the move had been removed from the backbone for ease of transportation. They had never been permanently fastened to the keel structure. They were just temporary placed there with the help of some of the men at the farm. There had been no funds to purchase the required bolts then, nor, was there now.

Currently the frames were stacked about one hundred and fifty feet behind the shop structure. The smallest, there were seven in all, was some ten feet wide, nine feet tall and with its temporary bracing structures weighted in at about three hundred pounds. The largest, the mid-ships frame, was eighteen feet wide, eleven feet tall, and weighed over five hundred pounds. The question was how was I to move these monsters some two hundred feet, then lift them onto the keel, erect them into a vertical level and plumb position, with just Debbie and myself? Even if all this could be done how could I fasten them and keep them in place with no bolts? I had forgot the Lord?

I stood there looking at the keel, "Lord," I said, "I am willing to do the work, but your going to have to show me how." I said out loud.

Instantly I knew how to accomplish the task. I ran to the house to tell Debbie what I had just been told and to ask her if she thought she could help me when I needed and extra hand. I went back outside and found and old well pulley, about twelve inches in diameter, we had acquired somewhere along the way, and attached it to the highest point possible on the stem of the keel structure. Next I threaded a length of nylon line through the pulley and around the structure I placed several eighteen foot 2x4's to be used as braces. At each frame station I nailed a block to act as a stop for the frame to rest against as it was raised into position.

All that remained was to move the frames to the keel. I decided to do this one at a time, erecting each one as it was brought to the keel. The midships frame was first since it was the largest and would be the most difficult to manage, requiring more room with nothing in the way.

I still did not know how I was going to move the frame to the keel, but I figured that since the Lord had shown me how to put the frames in place on the keel, He would also help me move it to where it belonged. I reached down and with all my strength, all I could muster, remember this thing weighs in excess of five hundred pounds, I lifted the frame. I almost fell flat on my back! The frame lifted as if it had no weight at all!

I moved it to the keel as if it was mounted on roller bearings, I was astounded. Upon reaching the keel I once more lifted it, more cautiously this time, on to the keel and made it ready to lift with no more effort than one uses with a sack of groceries from the car to the house. I was ecstatic! I quickly attached the rope and a couple of braces to the outer edges and called Debbie out to help. In less then five minutes we had raised the frame into place and had it braced. When I told her what had happened all I got was a knowing smile. God I hate it when she's right!

One hour later the remaining six frames were in place. All that remained to do was to make final alignment and leveling, This, however, could not be done until the frames could be securely fastened to the keel structure. This could not be done until the required bolts were purchased, and since these cost two hundred dollars including freight, a princely sum for us a the moment, they were not likely to appear anytime soon. Once again the work was at a stand still, or so I thought, and with all we had accomplished that day I was completely content to end the days efforts and begin again the next day.

The next morning I once again stood looking at the structure before me. Suddenly I knew how it could be done, at least temporarily, without the bolts. Quickly I found the commercial strapping tools remaining from our days of shipping products from the manufacturing operation. With just one or two abortive attempts, I discovered the proper procedure, and quickly bound the frames to the keel as securely as they would ever be once the permanent bolts were installed.

From that morning until the vessel was finished I began each day the same, standing looking at the structure asking the Lord what was to be done that day and how to do it. He never failed to tell me. Also from that day, I did no other work but the building of the S/ V Maranatha and the preaching of His word when allowed.

From the moment the frames were secured the work progressed as rapidly as possible since I was working by myself. But I must pause to qualify the phrase, "working by myself." I know it is simply a figure of speech, but in this instance not necessarily accurate. Aside from the obvious that as Christians we are told we are never alone, in my case working on the S/V Maranatha, I was never working alone literally.

During the months I spent building Maranatha, I cannot count the times I would catch movement out of the corner of my eye only to turn and find nothing there. I would turn back to my work only to realize that in that instant of looking away from my work, some small thing, some small task had been accomplished. Truly I was not alone for as I returned to work the movement once again became visible out of the corner of my eye.

I know there are those of you who will find this part hard to fathom, but I came to believe, that movement could only be the Lords angels sent to help me build His vessel. I soon learned to ignore the movement and the presence, whatever it might have been, was no longer momentary, but stayed with me as long as the work lasted each day. I cannot say that I ever physically saw one of my helpers, for if I looked they were gone, but if I paid attention to my work they worked steadily along side me.

Many times I would find myself doing a particular job only to realize that until that moment I had no knowledge of the need for the task or the skills required to accomplish it. I would marvel at the faithfulness of the one who had shown me and given me the knowledge to complete the task, even the knowledge that the job was required to be done.

I was truly a blessed man. I was never alone, for God had sent his hosts to help me, His child, to build the Maranatha.

The frames were aligned, plumbed, and leveled. They were braced securely in place and ready for the next step. Long flexible timbers called strakes, sixty five feet long to accommodate the curve of the hull from stem to stern, were constructed. The first to be installed were on either side of the chine, where the bottom curves up to become the sides. Two each on either side of the hull, one on the bottom and one on the side, together forming the chine log. Then at the top on both sides, another was installed which is known as the sheer strake. These last two form the outline of what would become the finished hull. The sheer strakes also formed the upper edge of the vessel where the deck would eventually be fastened.

Once these members were in place the basic hull shape was defined and became fairly rigid. Intermediate strakes were installed between the sheer and chine and chine and keel with the final member called the garboard strake being installed next to the keel on either side. The net effect of all this was a large open cage like structure showing the outlines of a rather large boat.

Since all of this was happening in full view of our neighbors and the whole world for that matter, we began to attract a lot of attention and visitors. I cannot remember the number of times I was asked if Noah was my father, or if I was indeed Noah returned. All were cheerfully received, even though at times they delayed the work. I took time to answer all their questions and gradually, as the days went by, most contented themselves with driving by on the weekends to see how the work was progressing. The traffic on our back country road increased considerably during our stay at Luther. We were at the time the little communities most infamous residents.

The next phase was construction of the ribs of the vessel, between the mold frames. Daily as the ribs were laid into place and fastened to the strakes the cage more and more took the shape of a very large vessel and it became easier to see or to visualize the completed vessel. It was possible to stand in just the right position and sight along the ribs so that the appearance was given of a solid structure, making it possible to see the beauty and curve of the finished hull.

Myself hanging on my ladder installing rib frames

I was extremely excited and happy. I knew in my heart of hearts I was exactly where I was supposed to be, doing what I was supposed to be doing, doing exactly what my whole life to that point had prepared me to do. I was an extremely happy man. I had a wonderful wife, whom I did not deserve. Work which totally fulfilled me, and a Lord who despite all my short comings, loved and walked with me daily. What more could a man ask for?

All was not roses, however. I do not want to paint too much of an idyllic picture. We no longer had a bank account, so the infamous seventy nine dollars was now a thing of the past. Debbie had gone to work as a night clerk at Circle K, so I did not see much of her. The money she made kept our bills paid and supplied us with food, but there was nothing left over. I had determined I would continue the building with what I had on hand, until nothing more could be done. It would then, as it had always been, be the Lord's responsibility to either supply the means to continue, or release me to find other work, and continue the work at a later time.

Don't you just love it, how I am always deciding what the Lord needs to do?

I also developed a sever reaction to the chemicals which made up the glues used in laminating the parts of the structure together. Even though I had taken every precaution to keep the substance from my skin I had developed a very sever rash on various parts of my body, mostly my hands, inner wrists, and upper legs. It was painful, irritated and itched maddeningly.

This allergy was not new though, we did not know it at the time, but had been latent in my system for many years. We found out years later, even though the doctors did not know when it started, they were certain this allergy was the basis of the difficulties I had while in the hospital in Guthrie so many years earlier when the horse kicked me.

The intense use of the epoxies brought on by the size and duration of the project greatly magnified the allergy. There were other side effects as well, among them dental problems, breathing, and even impotence. As the use of the epoxies increased so did the various side effects and their associated problems. We had no possibility of doctors or medicines, we had no insurance or the ability to pay any of the costs associated with them. Possibly the effects would not have been as strong and as long lasting, if there had been the ability to secure medical help, but there was not.

Also, for whatever reason the Lord choose not to deliver me from this ailment, as he had from others, so we continued to suffer from the effects of the allergy. Long hot baths were my only relief and at times even those offered no escape. The only solution was to discontinue use of the chemicals, however, this could not be done until the vessel was completed.

I to this day cannot use even the slightest amount of that material or related chemicals without sever reactions. Most of the effects lasted for months, others years, and some to this day, after the last epoxy was used. I have recovered from most of the long term effects of the prolonged use of the material, but needless to say I stay as far away from epoxies and related products as possible.

BILL

<hr>

We had continued to go the monthly pastors meeting zealously, because we had meet several people there who we respected and admired, and there never seemed to be the same group twice in a row. Attendance at these meetings helped to kept us abreast of the happenings in the church world while we were in our isolation.

After the meeting in April, we were conversing with a young Pastor who was the cousin of our Pastor Roger. He was pastor of a small congregation on the southeast side of Oklahoma City. During the course of our conversation he invited us to present our mission and the work to his congregation that following Sunday evening. We accepted gladly, since it was our first invitation to speak anywhere since beginning our disastrous association with the Grace Rescue House and the two Brothers.

We arrived at the church that Sunday evening hopeful but nervous. After the praise and worship session was completed I took the podium. As the sound man played a tape I had given him of Chariots' of Fire by Dino, I quickly moved through slides of our trip to the Islands some sixteen months earlier. I ended the slides with a picture of the sunrise on that last morning at sea when the Lord had spoken so clearly. As the last strains of music faded and I repeated the promise of that morning, the members of Harold's congregation were very silent and fixed solidly in their seats. I had no idea what to do next or how they had received us thus far. A frightening moment.

I continued, completing the presentation as quickly as possible, asking for questions as I ended. There were a few of the type one would expect about the people of the islands presented, how we expected to minister, and a few about the vessel we were building. I closed explaining where we were located, giving direction and extending invitations to all who would like to visit the construction site to see the vessel for themselves.

Afterward as we were packing up the projection equipment preparing to leave, the young pastor presented us with an envelope. He explained it contained the offering for that evening. He and the staff had decided it should be ours, we thanked him and departed to our car. As we started the car we realized we did not have enough gas to get home some thirty plus mile distant. We also had no money for gas. Remembering the envelope, I opened it to discover it contained a check drawn on the church account. We sat there not knowing what to do, finally I decided to go back and tell our dilemma to the pastor. This I did with some embarrassment. Much to my surprise he completely understood, explaining that in the early days of his ministry on the road, he often had to ask for the love offering to be in cash in order to buy gas and food in order to move on to his next service.

He graciously took the check and converted it to cash. Then he wrote another check, larger than the first from his own account, thus more than doubling our offering for the night. I was astounded and humbled. This was the first time in months I had admitted the true state of our finances to a fellow Christian and the response was immediate. I could not help but wonder what the results would have been had I taken this action months earlier, instead of standing firm in what I believed to be faith in the Lord.

Was I guilty of the sin of Pride? I certainly was guilty of failing to understand that we were surrounded by others, who while following their call from the Lord, struggled just as hard as we had through the difficulties the world and the church throws at us, in order to hinder our success. I had forgotten those called to ministry are also called to be Christs representatives to all the world, and also to the ones the enemy has sent to destroy His work. Why should we expect any less?

I was truly repentant as I explained what had happened to Debbie as we made our way toward home. By way of celebration, for the first time in a year, we stopped at a Braum's Ice Cream store and we each had a double dip of our choice. The Lord is so good to His kids when we let Him order our steps. That young pastor will never know how his reaction to our plight affected my walk of faith with the Lord.

The next morning found me as usual at work on the Maranatha. Working twenty feet above the ground on a shaky ladder fastening ribs to the strakes. This morning as I worked, I did so with a lighter heart, thinking of the events which took place on the evening before. On the way home, we had stopped at a twenty four hour grocery store and purchased some much needed supplies and for the first time in a very long time I had coffee with my breakfast that morning.

The work was going smoothly and I was reluctant to stop as I noticed a cream colored pickup truck with a very large propane tank mounted over the its cab turn into our drive. The truck came to a halt in a cloud of dust fifty or so feet from the spot where I clung precariously to my ladder.

The two occupants of this fascinating truck, with its fuel tank mounted over the cab, just sat there not moving or speaking to each other. Neither attempted to exit the vehicle. I eventually gathered my wits and descended to the ground. I had barley reached the ground when the passenger door opened and a lady I remembered from the night before exited from the truck. She introduced herself as Shirley and the driver of the truck as her brother Bill. Bill still sat there in the truck simply looking through the windshield at the structure standing before him.

Shirley explained she had been present at our presentation the night before. She had been so excited by our presentation she had hardly slept after returning to her home. Early that morning she had told her brother all about us and since she did not drive she had asked him to bring her out to us so she could see the "miracle," her words, with her own eyes. As she talked her brother, Bill, was silent sitting there in the truck, looking at the skeleton of the S/V Maranatha and I noticed tears in his eyes.

I apologized to Shirley and Bill, as he at last made his way out of the truck, that there was not more for them to see, but she would not hear any of it, declaring she could see Maranatha in all her glory, she was extremely excited. We talked for sometime with her and her brother taking it all in, finally I remembered to be hospitable and invited them in for coffee which they gladly accepted. As I served them the steaming liquid, I smiled to myself, remembering it was the first time in months we'd had coffee in the house. Bill began to ask questions and more questions concerning my plans. He asked how I proposed to accomplish them, where were the funds to come from and so on and on. I answered each as best I could and finally he asked, "at this time what is your greatest need?"

Without hesitation I answered, "bolts for the keel and an extra pair of hands."

He fell silent as I rolled up the drawings for the vessel which had been spread out on the floor. Finally he told Shirley they needed to leave as he must get back to his business. I thanked them for coming and invited them back anytime they wished to come and see our progress. As Bill walked to the truck he handed me some folded money stating,"maybe this will help with the bolt problem and I'll pray about the extra pair of hands. I also need to discuss this with my wife."

They both waved, as the pickup roared to life and in a cloud of dust, hustled its way down our curving bumpy driveway. As they disappeared over the hill I looked at the money folded in my hand. Unfolding it revealed two crisp one hundred dollar bills, exactly the amount needed to purchase the needed bolts including shipping. A figure I had not mentioned to Bill in our conversations of that day. A few minutes later Debbie arrived home from school. We were both very excited as I shared the events of my morning with her.

A few days later, shortly before lunch time I again was hanging from my ladder fastening ribs to the structure of the vessel when I saw that same pickup come roaring down the road and turn into our drive. I quickly made my way to the ground and met Bill as he got out of his truck. After the usual pleasantries were exchanged he asked if there were some place in town we could eat lunch. A short time later we found ourselves in a little country cafe located in the center of Luther. We ate a leisurely lunch, and as we ate, Bill told me his story.

Bill had been one of the original founders of the church where his sister Shirley now attended, and our pastors young cousin was now the pastor. He had since moved on, as changes had occurred, and he felt moved to seek fellowship in another place of worship. Bill was, as I was to learn, a man of deep conviction. He told me that when he first saw the ship, as he always referenced the Maranatha, he was over whelmed by the Holy Spirit and he knew he had to be a part of her construction.

He owned a business and had for the past twenty years been in the same location. His business was the re-manufacturer of refrigerators and other appliances, but mostly refrigerators. Though not a wealthy man, he stated, the Lord had been good to him and he could devote some of his time to work on the ship. He proposed to spend, if I accepted him, Wednesday afternoons and Saturday mornings working on the ship, as he needed to spend the rest of his time with his business and his wife Marge. I told him that was more than acceptable to me and that his assistance would be more than welcome.

The most startling revelation came next.

He explained he had a large storage yard at his place of business which was full of junked refrigerator bodies and other junked appliances. He also had a warehouse full of air conditioner coils and other salvaged copper and aluminum. He would donate all of this to us and provide the truck to haul it to the salvage yard if I would do the work. He was not sure but believed the salvage value to be around nine hundred to one thousand dollars. I, beside being dumbfounded, was overjoyed and accepted in the same manner. We made arrangements for the salvage work to begin the following week. I would go in with Debbie in the mornings and haul junk, returning home with her after classes. Bill took me home and to the Maranatha, stating as he left me standing there in a daze, that he would be back Saturday morning ready to work.

I spent the rest of the day in a daze not knowing what to do next. I waited anxiously for Debbie to get home so I could share the news of this particular day. I must admit, even though the news was exciting, we both developed a wait and see attitude. We had been promised so much before and led down a merry path by our fellow Christians only to be disappointed, or to find conditions imposed which were impossible to meet. We had become citizens of the show me state. Not a good frame of mind, but understandable non the less.

Bright and early the following Saturday morning I stood on my ladder and watched as that strange contraption, and the tank it held, roared up the road and into our drive, concealed in the now familiar cloud of dust, coming to a halt as the door opened and its driver emerged from the cloud.

Bill had arrived!

Maranatha's frame with Bill's truck in the fore ground

I must admit I was not prepared. For longer than I cared to remember I had only needed to concern myself with the work I myself was doing. I found it difficult to keep Bill occupied that first day, yet the time went quickly and promptly at noon he invited me and Debbie to lunch. We went to the cafe in Luther which was to become a weekly tradition during the next months. A time of fellowship and relaxation.

On Monday morning I found myself busily loading old refrigerators, with Bills help, into his stake bed truck. I do not remember the number we could haul at one time, but by the end of the morning I had collected one hundred eighteen dollars and change after paying for fuel. I was tired but excited. However, I found it hard to believe the junk I saw would come any where close to a thousand dollars. Bill assured me it would amount to that much, though I doubted, I none the less rejoiced in what we had no matter the amount.

As I completed the first day and parked the truck in anticipation of Debbie's arrival, I took the money I had collected to Bill, after all it belonged to him. I assumed that after the job was finished he would give me whatever he had intended to give from the proceeds.

I was heartened and surprised when he refused it stating it was mine, not his, he had given all the junk to the building of the ship. I then asked if he would mind if I used some of the first money to buy my wife a bible. She needed a new study bible very badly for school. I had not been able to purchase her anything for Christmas and I would like very much to get her a new bible. He seemed pleased as he told me, "The money is yours to spend as you feel the Lord leads."

Debbie was very surprised and happy when I asked her to stop at a bible store on the way home. I will always cherish the look in her eyes as she held the new bible in her hands and touched her name in gold on the cover.

Over the next ten days I hauled junk in the mornings and worked on Maranatha in the afternoons. When all the junk was sold I sat in our small kitchen with a cigar box full of money. Debbie and I were shocked to find, that when counted, the cigar box held one thousand eight hundred seventy eight dollars and change. Adding in the cost of fuel purchased and the cost of Debbie's bible the total sale of the junk had been just a few cents less than Two thousand dollars, twice the amount Bill had forecast. Bill was greatly surprised also when I told him a day or two later.

The funds thus gathered purchased plywood for the structural bulk heads and sub-deck, tongue and groove material for the overheads, material for the interior decking, the prop and shaft along with it's bearing fixture, and ballast materials. The engine was also purchased from these funds, but that is another chapter.

PROGRESS?

Bill was a wonder! Not only did he show up to work when he said he would, but he was always sneaking away from his business whenever possible. He also had the ability to solve some of the many problems which continually presented themselves.

For example, in order to install the propeller shaft a two and one half inch hole needed to be drilled through the deadwood portion of the keel. This is no big deal, after all the keel is made of wood right? Well is becomes a big deal when the length of the hole is five and one half feet. You do not find a drill bit of this length at the local hardware store! Bits for this purpose are available but they are extremely expensive. Bill after studying the problem one afternoon, returned the next day with a bit he had fabricated in his shop, and by the end of that day the hole was completed and ready for the installation of the shaft and it's fixtures.

Bill provided a wealth of equipment and knowledge in its use, he made his skill, knowledge, tools, and resources available to us for the construction of the ship. He even did what he could do to see that we were comfortable.

When the refrigerator in the trailer quit, he appeared the next day with one to replace it, that was nicer and newer than the one it replaced. When I told him I could not work one afternoon because I had to go to town with Debbie and do our laundry he appeared with a washer and dryer. We had to hook them up outside since there was no room in the trailer for them, but we had laundry facilities just outside our door. What a luxury! When the Oklahoma winter suddenly turned to summer, as it does, he arrived with an air conditioner for our use. He truly was a wonder and I found myself depending upon him more and more each day.

Due to the influx of funds from the junk money and Bill's energy the next few weeks saw a great change in the Maranatha. The structure of the skeleton was completed and now it was possible for anyone to see the form of the very large vessel taking shape on that Oklahoma hilltop. The traffic on the road increased steadily as those from all around drove by to check on the progress of the modern day Noah's ark being built in their community. At this point she was an impressive sight, the dull red mahogany of her structure seemed to glow warmly against the cold clear blue skies of the Oklahoma spring. The massive structure, standing two stories above her hilltop, was it seemed poised to set sail across the undulating prairie.

While the weather was still cold and the timing was correct in the building schedule, we began the installation of the ballast material. I do not remember the exact weight, but it was to be in excess of eight thousand pounds. We constructed a simple smelter using a burner from an old water heater and an iron kettle and began the process of melting and pouring the eight thousand pounds of molten metal, a combination of pot metal and lead, one ten pound ladle at a time, a back breaking process.

During this time Debbie invited her bible school class out for a picnic and we decided to make it an event. We invited everyone we thought might come and one Saturday in May had a picnic and a day of fellowship with our friends.

Everyone was duly impressed with the Maranatha and with the exception of a very windy day a good time was had by all. It was good to relax and enjoy a day of fellowship for a change. It was during this day that I met Vern and his wife Janice. Debbie had told me of him, as a second semester entrant to the Bible School, other than that I knew little of him.

The moment we were introduced the Lord spoke to me, and I knew they were brought to us to mentor and possibly to be crew members.

I have always made it a practice to keep these words of knowledge to myself to give them time to mature. I believe rushing to tell the person involved may unduly pressure and influence that individual, for good or bad, for if the word is truly from the Lord it will not go away or change with a little time. I wait for the Lord to speak a word to that individual, and then when they come to me, I already have confirmation. This time, however, as the day wore on I felt the need to at least invite them to join us in the work.

Finally, I gave in and approached them with the invitation. I tried to do this without revealing to them what the Lord had revealed to me concerning them. I wanted them to hear it from the Lord first. However, Vern would not let that happen and continued to question me and push for an answer until I reluctantly told them about the word I had received when I first met them. I have always wondered if I did the right thing in approaching them. Yet, as I relive the events in the writing of them, I wonder now if Vern had also received a word that he was attempting to understand?

Ultimately as it turned out, Vern and Janice joined our team a few days later. Vern began working with Bill and I, two or three afternoons a week, and Janice would be there on Saturdays. I must say here also, this was a situation Bill never quite accepted, he just was never comfortable around Vern for some reason. Vern's efforts always seemed to be a little halfhearted, and he was not dependable, possibly the reason for Bill's discomfort.

We began, sadly to say, to count on him when we saw him driving into the yard. Janice was just the opposite, she was excited and enthused about being part of such a project and put her whole effort into everything she was asked to do. She and Debbie developed a great friendship.

Work on the vessel progressed rapidly. The bulkheads and the sub-deck were installed, we had decided to construct the sub-deck believing it would provide some shelter as the spring and summer came on. I had also decided to install the hull bottom and as much as possible of the interior, leaving the sides of the hull to the last. By doing this the deck provided shade from the broiling sun, and the open sides allowed the breezes to flow through, providing a rough form of air conditioning.

This plan served us very well on that basis, but the deck did not keep out the rains, and as the bottom was installed keeping her dry became an increasing problem.

Debbie and I began to spend more and more time socially with Vern and Janice. We needed to become better acquainted if the subject of becoming crew members were to be proposed. We had learned a valuable lesson with our experience of the first crew and did not rush into an invitation this time. We enjoyed each others company and got along well, yet, Vern still seemed only half committed. I on the other hand began to have concerns about his dependability.

I could not shake the feeling that when the chips were down I would not be able to count on him. At sea in a small boat, and despite her size to us Maranatha was a small boat, one must have assurance that every member of the crew can be relied upon. In an emergency there is no time for discussion or halfhearted efforts. The environment of the oceans, will and have, risen up and slapped many a halfhearted sailor into oblivion, along with his ship and fellow crew mates. Vern and Janice continued with us, yet, I knew that one way or another the problem would resolve itself. In August it did!

Vern during his youth and early twenties had been heavily involved in drugs and had turned to crime to support his habit. He eventually was apprehended and sent to prison for life as an habitual criminal. During his incarceration he had a genuine salvation experience and through his new relationship with the Lord Jesus Christ his life was changed. A few years later as a result of this change he met Janice through an outreach ministry to the prison. A year later his sentence was commuted and he was released from prison. A short time later he and Janice were married.

While he was in prison he had received ordination through an organization which works mostly with prisons. Like most, if not all, who find themselves in trouble with the law Vern had a problem with authority, any authority. This I was to learn was the reason behind his halfheartedness. To his credit, he did battle the problem and worked to overcome it. Unfortunately he did not understand he could not win the victory by himself and never surrendered the problem to the Lord for solution. This is very understandable since the root of the problem is submission of any sort.

My ordination through Faith Christian Fellowship International was still on a provisional basis as I had not yet served the full time required in provisional status that was required prior to full accreditation. I learned that because of this Vern considered himself superior to me. Therefore, he believed himself to not be subject to my authority as head of Spirit Wind Ministries. This was the root of my lack of confidence in his commitment to our project.

In late August a situation arose in which I asked, as head of the ministry, that he not participate. I believed participation in this particular event would reflect badly upon the ministry. He refused to do as I asked and stated point blank that I had no right to interfere in his affairs. He was a great fan of Kenneth Copeland so I used the following example in an effort to explain my position.

"Vern," I said, "if you had joined the staff of Copeland's ministry instead of ours, and a similar situation had arisen in which Kenneth had asked you not to participate, especially in your ministerial capacity, with Kenneth acting in the authority as the chose head of the ministry to which you have submitted, would you still insist upon carrying out this action against his wishes?"

"Of course not!" He stated.

"Well that being the case, why is it any different here? I am the head of this ministry under the Lord. I feel this action would be detrimental to the ministry and in that capacity I have asked you to refrain from involvement in this one thing. Why in this case am I any different than Kenneth Copeland?"

"Well your not ordained and I am." He declared.

"However, I am the appointed leader of this ministry and hold that capacity as ordained by the Lord. My ordination from men is just a technicality and is to be completed when all the ordaining organizations requirements are met. Truthfully I can see no difference." I stated. "Vern, I believe if you insist in taking part in this situation which may bring harm to this ministry, against my wishes, you cannot continue to be a part of this ministry." Truthfully, I regretted the words as I spoke them, but knew there could be no other course.

"Well," he said as his face brightened, "I will have to pray about it." He turned and walked away.

We did not see him for a few days after that, but I knew the outcome, for I had given him the out he needed in order to quit without guilt.

One evening after Bill had gone home, Vern and Janice drove into the yard. We invited them in and as Debbie served everyone tea, Vern announced they would no longer be part of our project. He said he could not be part of a ministry that restricted him in any way. In the end the only authority he felt he could or would recognize over him would be that of the Lord Himself. I was not surprised at his attitude, I was very concerned for him, I knew that without submission to the covering authority of others within the body of Christ, a person standing alone is vulnerable to attack from any direction and of also falling into error at any turn.

Vern's refusal to submit to my authority as head of the ministry was in itself important only in its effect on Spirit Wind Ministries. Much more serious and of greater concern to Debbie and I, and as we discovered his wife Janice, was the extent to which rebellion against authority still maintained control over Vern's thoughts and actions.

We all expressed these concerns, but he would not or could not hear us. Finally I accepted their withdrawal with reluctance. I had realized during our conversation that the purpose for Vern's being placed with us was for him to gain disciplines necessary for him to control his rebellion. I, in my ineptitude, had missed it and could only pray the next person the Lord placed in his path would have better insight than I had exhibited. I pray that, whoever that person may be, they can help Vern to achieve the victory he and Janice deserve.

Debbie and I were very deeply saddened as they departed that evening. We missed them already. Debbie had graduated from the Bible school in June and shortly after this event the Lord moved us to another church. We never saw them again.

CHURCH CHEAP

The summer months of 1986 were wonderful, even with all the problems which occurred. The Maranatha grew steadily on the hill in central Oklahoma. True my allergies to the epoxy grew worse, Vern and Janice came and went, and funds while more plentiful were ever a problem.

Bill had become more and more deeply involved and also was becoming more demanding. He was determined to see the vessel completed as fast as possible, regardless of details I had been given through the vision. He insisted more often on doing things his way regardless of the vision.

Yet, the vessel was being born before our eyes on a red clay hilltop in the middle of the Oklahoma prairie. It was a magnificent summer!

**Myself and a friend standing on a portion of the
deck shortly before the bottom was in stalled.
All of the interior bulk heads are in place but not yet completed.**

I made a mistake during that summer which I think is not uncommon to those in ministry. In our case the results of that mistake would indeed prove costly and at times dangerous.

Bill had began to take charge of more areas of the project, eventually insisting things be done his way or not at all. In effect it became his ship and it's completion possessed him. My mistake was deferring to him in the beginning, after all I did not know how to do many of the things necessary to build the vessel. However, Bill seemingly did, I had had the vision and had seen the details, but Bill had the means to accomplish them. It was after all his money we were using, but it was more than money, Bill had the ability to get many things done I did not. My mistake was in allowing Bill to assume a role to which he was not entitled.

The weeks went by and more and more of his money and efforts were spent on the vessel, and I found myself deferring to him and his will, especially in areas where the vision had not been clear. The danger in this, as I now know, is that in rushing the completion of details not yet made clear, we were substituting our wisdom and solutions, sometimes Bill's and sometimes mine, for those of the Lord. A situation I believe all of us find ourselves in from time to time.

I find it difficult to express myself in this matter for during the time I spent with Bill that summer I grew to love him deeply and still do. He became the older brother I had never had, the older brother all eldest children wish they had. My temptation is to gloss over the rough parts and ignore the less than stellar parts of our relationship. However, if I were to do that I would not be painting a true picture of the life one assumes when one sets out to follow a vision of the Lord faithfully.

Bill became such an important part of our lives I find it very difficult to impart any negativity to his part in the project and our story. I can only say that had I a little more experience and been a stronger leader none of it would have happened. It is a problem I pray about continually to this day and a burden which continues to plague my heart.

The engine is a case in point. In the days following the junk sale there was much discussion between Bill and myself about the auxiliary engine to be installed in Maranatha's bowels. The Lord had been silent on this point and with hind sight I am not sure there was even supposed to be one installed, but that is another story.

After much research into the matter I had finally settled upon a Volvo Marine conversion, being marketed by a company named VETUS, in this country. It was a complete system supplying everything required for the installation of a power system in a vessel the size of Maranatha. It was also a diesel which was an absolute requirement. It's cost including freight would be five thousand five hundred dollars give or take a few dollars. No small matter. I was not concerned, because we were many weeks away, even possibly months, from being pressed to install the engine. The only pressing need was to determine the size of the engine and it's components in order to properly size the engine compartment.

Bill on the other hand was in a near panic about the engine. He insisted we needed to settle the matter now, not later. He also was against the very thought of spending over five thousand dollars on one item. I explained in detail it was not just one item but an entire system that included the engine, raw to fresh water cooling, charging system, gearbox, prop and shaft connections, and so on, but he was not convinced.

One afternoon a week or ten days after our last discussion on the matter and the sale of the junk, he arrived with the news he had found an engine for us. I needless to say was surprised. He further explained he had found a small diesel at a salvage yard operated by a friend of his. It was an automotive diesel and was still in it's 1982 Opel automobile. The car had been totaled from behind and had only eighteen thousand miles showing on the odometer, so it should be in great shape. The best part, according to Bill, was it could be ours for only two hundred fifty dollars. He was beside himself with excitement, I was not!

I tried to explain the difference between a marine engine and the automotive type. For one thing the transmissions are totally different, they mount in a different manner, and the automotive transmission is useless in the marine environment. Radiator cooling systems are also worthless, deep inside a vessels hull, where the cooling air moving across the radiator is lacking. The exhaust systems are not jacketed to be cooled with water in order to reduce the heat radiated into the interior of the vessel and reduce the possibility of fire. The problems are many and costly to properly correct, especially on a one off basis. Bill would hear none of it.

"I can build all that stuff myself," he flatly stated, "I don't see why we should spend all that money if we can make do with less!" These are the most disastrous words in the American church, "make do."

During my days as an Architect, before and after my conversion, I refused to take on church projects for just that reason. During those days I called it "Church Cheap." I never understood why people, who in their own personal lives insisted upon the very best money could buy, when placed upon a church committee would insist the best God deserves is equipment and conditions they themselves would only consider sending directly to the dump, and totally beneath consideration for their own use.

Church cheap! I hate it and have zero tolerance for it, yet here I was face to face with it staring me in the eye, in the person of Bill and his engine.

The mistake? After several days of his insistence and assurance he could do the conversions required, I relented.

The little Izuzu diesel engine was extracted from it's cradling Opel automobile to become the largest pain in the lowest vertebrae in my spinal column for years to come.

This all took place in April and it was a cold rainy day in November when the engine itself was hoisted aboard and lowered into place deep within the hull. It was the following March, almost a full five months later, before the engine ever sputtered into life. Not including Bill's labor, the parts and materials required to complete the installation of the little Izuzu/Opel automotive engine, was five thousand seven hundred twenty five dollars and fifty cents, and yet we still did not have a dependable marine power plant.

So much for church cheap!

It has been my experience that this misguided effort to make do, always costs more than it saves, and replacement later usually comes at a time when it can least be afforded. In this case three years later, when I finally was forced to throw the engine on to the junk heap, it's replacement engine alone cost three thousand three hundred dollars and two months time in the marina. Money we had been saving for years to allow us to continue our journey. An added cost of the engine saga was that the replacement of this Izuzu/Opel piece of junk came as close as anything ever has to ending Debbie's and my marriage.

How great the cost of church cheap!

Once I awakened to the developing problem, the dye had been cast and it became increasingly difficult to control and maintain the quality, I knew would be required of a vessel once she put to sea. Bill was as I have said a genius at solving problems, his one fault lie in his refusal to accept any difference in the severity of environs, between the land and the sea.

I am sure most of the systems he constructed, would if used properly and entirely on land based applications, would last for years, but they just did not match those required for sea. Gradually, I did not resist and I must admit initially it appeared as if his solutions would work, even though my gut knew better. Usually, since I could not be in two places at once, I would discover Bill's changes after the fact when it was too late or to costly to start over.

In July as we started to apply the bottom sheathing, my allergy to the epoxy was so sever I elected to let Bill and Verne do all to work gluing the bottom together. This would allow me to completely remove myself from direct contact with the glue. I spent one afternoon showing them how to apply the glue and the overlapping pieces of sheathing plywood, in order to achieve a proper bond, and not have what is termed as dry joints or voids.

The next afternoon Bill and Vern were busy installing the bottom starboard side from forward to midships. I was relieved to be away from the glue, and they, from their conversations I could hear as they worked, seemed to be doing very well with the work. The bottom consisted of six layers of quarter inch plywood laminated to each other and fastened securely to the ribs and the strakes. The strength of the system depended upon a continuous bond between the layers of plywood with a minimum of void. This was essential.

The only way to insure a void free system was to use an excess of glue and the fasten each piece from the center outward working the excess to the edges. If done properly the result was no voids, extreme strength, and little waste, as the excess glue squeezed out was used to seal the edges of the plywood. All of this had been explained and demonstrated the day before, and its importance I thought, understood by Bill and Vern.

Imagine my consternation, when on a trip to the ground for some reason, I noticed the plywood they were lifting into place appeared to be dry without glue. I stopped them and asked abruptly what they were doing. I was informed by Bill that he had decided we were using to much glue and had therefore squeegeed all the excess off as he had determined it was not necessary. I was furious. Yet, I did not lose my temper, a minor miracle. I just ended all the work for the day and made an effort to determine how many pieces of plywood had been installed in that manner.

The epoxy had by this time set on all the pieces installed and the only way to remove them was to remove the entire bottom from midships forward. This could be done, but could prove very destructive to the overall strength of the boat. I decided to locate all the voids by sounding and pressure. Then drill into them and inject epoxy into the cavity, thus filling them and hopefully completing the bond between the pieces. Even though I could not be assured of finding all the voids I hoped enough could be found to avoid pulling the bottom off, destroying the expensive plywood, and starting over.

In any event my brief escape from the epoxy was over, since my two helpers had proven they could not be trusted to follow instructions. A few days later, after many hours of hunting and filling voids, I was satisfied enough had been corrected to allow work to continue and the balance of the bottom completed.

Bill was severely angered by this event, and for some time afterward was very short tempered, and quick to maintain I was wasting material. Gradually he cooled down and a normal peace descended upon the project. The voids not found would one day come back to haunt me and for that I have only myself to blame, because I should have insisted upon the removal of the incorrectly installed portion of the hull and started over, hang the expense and turmoil.

There are many more examples of this miserly attitude which plagued us. Bill as the weeks had gone by had expended a large amount of time and money on the project and I deferred to him in most matters. That is a very very large mistake. Never ever defer to anyone when you know another way is right for your vision or ministry. Latter after we had departed Oklahoma, one by one and usually at great expense, each one of Bills economies had to be replaced. Eventually only those hidden within the structure itself, and unknown to me, remained. These proved to be deadly.

I have only myself to blame, I was in charge, only my weakness allowed these things to occur. My warning to those of you in ministry, is to be vigilant and not allow this to happen in your ministry. Just because Aunt Minnie donates the majority of the funds for the remodeling of the fellowship hall, does not give her the right to demand the carpets be those salvaged from the Elks Lodge basement.

To all you Aunt Minnie's out there and to all of us everywhere, when we as Christians give of the monies and blessings the Lord has provided, we have given it to God and all claim, if indeed there ever was one, to the disposition and use of that gift is forfeited. At the moment of giving, responsibility for the use of that gift transfers into a relationship that is only between the recipient of the gift and God. If you have not the faith in the recipient to believe the gift will be use as God wishes, do not give it in the first place. Once given you no longer have a voice in the disposition of the gift once it has been made.

The responsibility falls upon those who have received your gift, for it comes from God through you. It is God who will judge the fitness of it's use, and He who will exact retribution, if it is improperly used.

SPIRITUAL COVERINGS

There are times when the responsibilities of the ministry you are given become like a mill stone around your throat.

Such was the feeling around the end of summer and early fall of 1986. True the work had gone well, Bill and Vern had been the extra hands I needed to progress this far. Bill's tireless work on the vessel and his money, which he continued to pour into it's construction, kept the work going at a non stop pace. The difficulties and differences of opinion, to that point at least, had been overcome or ignored. The S/V Maranatha stood there in all her glory, very much the image of the vessel she was to be, even minus her top hamper. Yet something was missing!

Debbie and I had been carrying the weight of Spirit Wind Ministries and the Maranatha virtually by ourselves since our marriage just two years earlier. We had accepted the task wholeheartedly and would not have stopped for any reason. A great strain had been placed on our relationship and both of us would at times look toward the Maranatha and wish she was not there. Yet, she always was there, asking more in the way of time, money, and attention. I remember a conversation Debbie and I had, both of us stating it seemed she never would be finished, she would just go on forever, demanding more and more. We felt at times there never would be any relief. Do not misunderstand, neither of us would have quit the mission, however, we were very tired and weary. At those times when we allowed our weariness to surface it seemed we were completely alone in the world and so very weary.

Even though we had worked hard, we still had no group to provide the covering we so desperately needed. There was no body to provide the umbrella of protection we so needed. Debbie and myself were required to do all the physical as well as the spiritual work. There was no group to intercede in prayer, turning aside the attacks of the enemy. We had to stand in the gap ourselves. This combined with the physical work required over these many months had simply worn us out.

Mentioned before is my belief that no ministry or individual, for the matter, can stand alone. There must be a spiritual covering to survive and prosper. This covering is provided for most people, if they are fortunate, by their local congregation. This is a function which is not too popular with most Americans, and therefore, is not discussed much in our assembled bodies.

We Americans are fiercely independent and wrongly interpret the spiritual covering of the church as interference in our lives. I know this can be the case, but when administered correctly, the spiritual covering given by an active body of Christ is a real blessing. It is also absolutely essential! In the protection of our independence we always seem to react in the extreme and brook nothing which even hints at interference in our lives. I think this one factor accounts for the vast majority of church hopping, church splits, and the constant moving of pastors by their respective groups.

We all, as part of our sense of self, need some place to call home. Home provides an anchor for our identity. Spiritual covering provides this ingredient in our spiritual lives. It gives us structure and support, a place where we belong.

Every ministry must have this same covering, to keep it from standing alone, to provide for intercession, and to reduce the possibility of drifting into error. This was the thing which was missing, yet, not for a lack of trying on our part.

Unlike Nehemiah as he rebuilt the walls of Jerusalem, Debbie and I had no one to stand in the gaps, and we had grown tired and beaten up while filling the gaps, and building the wall. In the very beginning Debbie and I had sought this covering knowing it to be essential. The Lord had sent us to several bodies and we approached them with the ministry and our need for acceptance and spiritual covering. In each case we were welcomed and we believed we had found our home, so to speak, but as the days and weeks went by we discovered the acceptance and support required were not in evidence. Then the Lord would move us to another body with instructions to, "shake the dust from our feet." we felt like Gypsies during this time. In each case we would discover later, the ministries and congregations involved, would experience downturns in their fortunes shortly after our departure.

Two of the churches involved ceased to exist, some of the pastors moved on to other endeavors in difficultly, and in all cases a "dying" seemed to take place.

I do not suggest that Spirit Wind Ministries and it's rejection was by itself the cause of all this, yet, I do suggest and believe we were part of a testing by the Lord of these various ministries to which we were sent. With our departure it appears the Holy Spirit no longer contended with them and they moved into a time of judgment. One pastor announce from his pulpit, on several occasions, that we were doing a great work and our ministry was worthy of support. He stated that their church was proud to be supporting us financially and spiritually. Yet, to the day of this writing Spirit Wind Ministries has never received a financial donation, nor has anyone connected with it been so much as spoken to by a person in leadership of that church.

I wondered as I contemplated those statements, then and now, at the definition of support used by that particular pastor. Another pastor, invited us on several occasions to speak at his church, as prelude to our covering being provided by that particular congregation. Each time we arrived it was as if we had never met and we were totally ignored. We would sit in the congregation waiting for him to introduce us and slowly realize the time to do so had passed and once more face the fact that he had not kept his promise. I rejected the next invitation, much to his surprise.

Finally once more in September we found ourselves on the doorstep of our old home church. A full circle had been accomplished and the Lord brought us back to our first home, we were, to say the least cautiously excited. Debbie and I remained quite and reserved about the work we were doing and the Maranatha. We just wanted to be in church and not be seen as some type of celebrity or kook by those around us. Most of all we were excited by the reception given to us by some of our old friends, especially Ed and Ruth Green.

It was not the same church we had left almost two years earlier, and we did not approach it the same either, this time we knew we were a test, and that they were about to be given an exam.

Under it's founding pastor, our church, had always been an introverted church. It was not at all, not in the least to the knowledge of the membership, involved with mission outreach of any type. The church direction was always inward to itself. I will always believe had the church been directed to extrovert itself, sending out missions, reaching out to the world, nothing could have stopped its growth.

The church to which we returned was different, many of the faces were the same, but the fire and spice were not there any longer. A new pastor was in charge, there was enormous debt, and the people in some respects had lost their drive and faith in the future of their church. Wrongly, most of the people had placed to much of their faith in the founding pastor, and when he departed, because their faith rested in him rather than the Lord, they were lost.

The new pastor worked hard to correct this and regain the drive that had been our church, but he did not have the charisma of the previous pastor, and it was just not working. Not long after our return a program was instituted to begin a mission outreach. There were to be special offerings taken over several Sundays, and the funds were to be set aside to fund various mission programs for one year beginning in January 1987. The special offerings were taken during October and November, and as the congregation that met each Sunday still numbered several thousand, the mission fund was well funded by the end of the offering period.

Upon our returning Debbie and I had requested, through a friend of ours who was still on staff, a meeting with the current pastor in order to present the ministry and our mission to him. We had asked to be sent forth, when the time came, as a church sponsored outreach, supported spiritually, doctrinally, and if possible financially. This had been our procedure in the past and we were sure it was the reason for our return to our church. We finally had our meeting in December, pastor listened attentively and told us as the brief meeting ended, he would discuss it with the staff and get back to us as soon as possible. I must admit we departed his office with troubled hearts, fearing rejection. We did not wish to once again depart from a church "shaking the dust from our feet," as we had done on so many occasions.

Some months earlier we had joined a study and support group which met weekly and was sponsored by the church. The group we joined was varied with people from all walks of life and backgrounds, as well as ages, however, all were married couples. In many ways the group served as a miniature church, adding the personal touch sometimes lost in a body as large as our church. The group was lead by a man named, Frank. We learned Frank worked for the State and was rather important in Oklahoma state law enforcement.

Debbie and I had decided going in that we would avoid telling the group about our work and ministry as we only wanted fellowship. We had discovered once people found out, we were in "ministry," everything changed in their relationship with us. We were no longer Debbie and Ken, and we desperately needed to be Debbie and Ken, if even for only a little while. Due to Frank's years in law enforcement, and the suspicious nature that develops, it was impossible to keep the ministry and the Maranatha secret and shortly everyone knew, not only the small group, but the entire church. Immediately the difference was there, and also because they knew we would be leaving soon, we never really became part of the group. These folks were to play several roles, and two or three individuals had important roles to play, as the Maranatha was completed and moved to water.

The pastor finally committed to financial support, but stopped short of committing to providing the church covering, and sending us forth as a church mission. The funds were to be provided at the rate of one hundred thirty dollars per month for one year and would be taken from the mission fund established by the special offerings. The money never came, and some months later we learned the mission fund had been dissolved. The funds were used for payment on the church debt. By this time we had been away from Oklahoma for several months.

Not receiving the promised funds did not effect us, even though they could have been put to good use, for we had long since learned not to depend upon the Church to live up to its promises. We had also long since turned our attentions to the work we were doing and as time passed all connections with our original church, the church where Debbie and I had started, were eventually lost. We never returned to the church where this story began.

Basically at Christmas time 1986 we found ourselves without the church covering we felt and believed we needed.

The S/V Maranatha was nearing completion and plans were being made for our move to water. We anticipated this to take place in January 1987. There remained many things to complete, but work was going well and we looked forward to our move. At Christmas time, we had sent a card to Lowrie and Judy, in hope it would reach them. We had no idea where they were and mailed the card to the last known address we had for them.

On one sunny afternoon in January, Bill, Debbie, and I were taking a break, when to my joy, I saw Lowrie and Judy walk past the living room windows. I jumped up, ran to the door pulling it open and hugging Lowrie and Judy almost in the same motion. The card had found them and they had found us.

Debbie and I were overjoyed as we welcomed them to our home. They were full of questions about the many many months that had passed since we had last seen each other. They were also very excited about the Maranatha resting behind the trailer. The last time Judy had seen her, she existed only as lines upon the lofting floor. Now she was complete, awaiting only for the ground to dry sufficiently to allow the move to water.

We introduced Bill, who had retreated to the background in the face of our enthusiastic greeting, and took them both on a tour of the Maranatha. Lowrie had been transferred to a church on the south side of Oklahoma City in the area known as Capital Hill. They had been there since early summer and really liked their new assignment. Lowrie asked if he could bring the youth group and it sponsors, out to see the Maranatha, and if we could come to the church to visit and speak to them concerning our mission. It was decided that due to our immanent departure, this all should happen on the next Sunday which was just a few days away. We spent a couple of hours exchanging the events of our lives and as they departed for home Debbie and I both had lighter hearts.

Bill, however, was not happy, he was even less than impressed with the fact that Lowrie was a Methodist minister, and was not in the least impressed by the prospect of our plans for Sunday. His attitude was at best a downer as he could see no good coming from our association with Methodists.

I ignored him since my association with Lowrie and Judy had nothing to do with the fact they were in the Methodist ministry, but rather, long years of friendship and brotherhood in Christ outside of our denominations.

Judy had become my sister in place of the one I had never known and Lowrie was my brother. They were my family, and to Debbie they were my half of the marriage, filling in for in-laws not present from my side of the family. In short they were beloved family, Bill could not or would not accept this fact, to him they were just Methodists, a threat to his Pentecostal way of thinking. I realized some years later this marked the beginning of Bill's removal from the project and our lives.

Debbie and I made our preparations, we cleaned and polished until the old trailer house sparkled. We also removed all the construction rubble from around the vessel and had her shipshape inside and out. This was to be the first time we were to receive visitors and we wanted her to look her best.

Sunday afternoon arrived quickly and we stood together anxiously as we watched several vans and cars turn into our drive and come to a stop in our yard. These were our family and the impression we made upon their congregation was very important to us.

The youth tumbled excitedly from the vehicles, yet, were no more excited than the adults accompanying them. I do not remember the exact number but there were thirty or more people crowding around

Debbie and I as we made them welcome. Lowrie introduced us to them, and during the next two hours we conducted groups up the ladder to give the tour, while answering hundreds of questions as youth and adults alike excitedly examined the vessel. They were full of enthusiasm for our project and we enjoyed them very much. It might sound strange, but no stranger than other things I have written here, but I could feel Gods pleasure with them and their excitement over His vessel. The Maranatha enjoyed them as much as they enjoyed her.

We traveled with them as they returned to Oklahoma City to the fellowship dinner prior to the evening meeting. By the time Debbie and I had started home that evening we had spent several wonderful hours with these folks, answered thousands of questions, but most importantly we had been accepted as family and the legitimacy of our calling had not once been questioned.

This is something we had not received from our meetings with the "spirit filled" body. Debbie and I returned home that evening refreshed and light of heart. The folks at Capital Hill United Methodist Church, had unknown to them, given us a much needed Spiritual lift. We took away with us much more than we left behind. At the time, unknown to us, we had met the portion of Christ's Church which was to give us the spiritual covering and support we so desperately needed.

"MYSTERIES AND NUMBERS"

During the summer and fall of 1986 while the Maranatha was being built many events, large and small, took place which can only be explained by placing them in a box labeled miracles. If I were to delineate all of them in this writing this work would increase in size exponentially. Not the least of these happenings was the fact that from the day Debbie and I raised the first mold frames to their places on the keel, and until we moved the Maranatha to the water, there were always materials on hand with which to build.

Also even though we did not at times see it, enough money, was always there to provide for our need. True our old car, Debbie's faithful Cutlass was on its last legs, but the Lord somehow kept it running. We did not eat out often, but our cupboards were stocked with good honest food. All and all the Lord took very good care of us, and true to His word, we really lacked for nothing.

The Maranatha truly was a blessed thing. She continued to grow daily before our eyes, becoming a beautiful and almost living thing. Daily we were impressed by her size and stature as she rested upon her red Oklahoma hilltop. I would stand upon her decks in the morning as the sun rose awakening us for another day, and I could almost feel her come to life, wanting to sail out across the sea of the undulating Oklahoma landscape. Two events took place during this time which are typical of those which took place daily and I will tell of them here.

One Friday afternoon in early fall I was working by myself down in the bilges of the vessel. The hull was about two thirds complete. The deck and bottom had been completed and the sides were installed from just forward of midships and from the stern forward stopping just even with the engine compartment. Most of the interior was installed in its rough unfinished form.

Deck looking forward from midships

Deck looking aft from mid ship
These two pictures were taken just prior to the event described below.

We were setting things in order, to finish the sides in the next few days, thus completing the hull. I was looking forward to this as a bench mark moment. I knew that much work would remain before she was complete, but when the holes in her side were filled Maranatha, would be for the first time the vessel, we had worked so hard to bring into being.

Debbie was late returning from work as she had gone to pick my daughter Mandy for her weekend visit. I finished the task I was working on and climbed down out of the hull just as they drove into the yard. They joined me as I cleaned my hands, admiring the vessel and talking of the progress made since Mandy's last visit. We decided to go in as a small thunderstorm popped up and seemed to be moving our way. The rains broke just as we entered the house.

I stood there looking out the window unable to see the vessel some fifty feet distant from me. The storm stopped as quickly as it started, with the sky immediately clearing and returning to a clear autumn evening. The rain had lasted no more than ten minutes, but the ground surrounding the vessel was covered with four to six inches of water. Water was running in torrents down the hill and underneath the vessel and her supports.

Suddenly I heard, rather than saw, her begin to move. Then I saw her move, slowly at first, as she began to slide backwards. Then very quickly the blocks and ground underneath her gave way and she slid off her cradling supports rolling over on to her starboard chine. The opening I had crawled out of only minutes before was now only inches above the ground as she came to rest with a rather heart rending crunch.

Suddenly, the deck loomed before us as an enormous vertical wall, cliff like in its proportions. Everything that had been resting on the flat surface just moments earlier was flying through the air as if pitched from the back of a rodeo bull. The table saw, which was on the deck, came to rest in the mud only a few feet from the trailer house with a loud thud. I knew in my heart it was ruined, yet, at the same instant I was grateful it had missed the house.

We all ran outside filled with emotions I still to this day can not identify with names. We stood there for a moment in shock looking at a disaster. Water was pouring out of the hull and bilge trough the opening in the side. I began to access the damage, while trying to determine just what had happened. I soon discovered that the rain had only fallen in a circle of roughly three hundred feet in diameter, centered directly over the Maranatha.

The hatch openings in the deck, not yet completed with their coverings, had allowed the hull to fill completely with water, adding tons of weight to her supporting structure almost instantly. At the same time the flood softened the ground beneath the supports allowing them to give way. This allowed the structure and all the water within to move, and once it started, nothing could stop it.

Laying there on her side she looked enormous and it was difficult to determine the extent of any damage. Yet, miraculously there seemed to be little. The cabinets which I had just framed in the galley had been wiped out by the cold plate, which was waiting to be installed in the freezer. The cold plate weighed almost one hundred pounds and as it slid across the cabin sole every thing in its path was damaged. It came to rest as it dug into a bulkhead between the galley and the cargo hold. The chine had come to rest in the mud and with the exception of one break where it had landed on a short piece of 2×4, it was undamaged. The greatest problem facing me at the moment was how to right the hull once more in order to repair damage and complete the building.

The problem was this; even in her unfinished state Maranatha was a weighty girl. I do not know exactly, but I estimated her weight then at eighteen tons. At her launching she weighed in at twenty six tons, and fully rigged ready for sea just under thirty tons. So on that Friday evening I was faced with the problem of raising a structure sixty feet long, eighteen feet wide, and sixteen feet deep, weighing some thirty six thousand pounds off the ground and back onto its supports. It needed to be tilted up to once again balance upon its keel and it's cradle.

I called Bill to tell him what had happened and that there would be no work to do until we put her back on her keel. I must have been in shock for it never occurred to me that Bill would be in the least bit concerned or interested. My only thought was to let him know he could not work on the boat as usual the next morning.

Thirty minutes later Bill's pickup came flying into the yard and came to a sliding halt in the mud a few feet from the looming deck. Bill just sat there in his truck with a look of hurt and surprise on his face. He was extremely upset with me for not calling him as soon as the accident had happened. I explained to him that I had called as soon as I could, but he did not comprehend, that the event had happened less than an hour earlier. He seemed to think something that catastrophic had to have taken a long time to occur. It was hours before he fully understood what had taken place and days before he ceased to blame me.

After some discussion we determined we would sleep on the problem of recovery. We would begin the next morning to try and solve the problem of righting the vessel and making a proper evaluation of the damage. The obvious solution of hiring a crane was out of the question because of finances. The travel time required to move a crane large enough to do the job, plus the hourly rate we estimated would be in the vicinity of a thousand dollars, funds we simply did not have. Therefore, we would be required to do it ourselves and at the moment we both were at a loss.

We had forgotten the Lord!

The next morning bright and early Bill and Vern arrived, as I stood with my morning coffee gazing at the "wreck," talking to the Lord the way I started every morning. Usually I was standing up on the deck gazing into the east, but this morning I was on the ground looking at the cliff like expanse of her deck as it rose vertically before me.

Bill had brought with him a couple of large house moving jacks and two or three come-a-longs. He had no other idea or plan other than simply to see if we could move the structure upright with the jacks while some how controlling it with the come-a-longs, some ropes and cables.

After some discussion about where to place the equipment, it was agreed we should give it a try, since at this point we had no other ideas and it seemed nothing to lose by trying. We set about our work discussing as we went the procedure we would use and the possible outcomes. I remember there was a concern that if we did manage to raise her as she neared the original position she might just keep on going and just simply roll onto her other side. We fastened some lines to her in an effort to prevent this from happening, though had that happened, in truth they could not have prevented it. Within two or three hours we had the jacks in place and all the equipment placed. We were ready to begin.

The first thing we had done was to place timbers under the keel for it to rotate onto and rest upon when the hull was righted. This was relatively easy to do as the hull rested almost totally on it's side raising the bottom and the keel some eighteen inches from the ground at the closest point. We then moved to the side laying on the ground to begin lifting.

I do not know if we were still acting in shock or if our faith was just that strong but we never, as you might expect, gathered in prayer to ask what to do or for help, we just began to do the work required. I do know however, that individually a lot of prayer was happening, both from us and Debbie and Mandy as they watched us.

We held our breaths as the first few rounds were turned on the house jacks and the weight of the hull came upon the timbers we had placed between the jacks and the surface of the hull. We had placed timbers there to spread the forces, we knew would be placed upon the hull, as the jacks were raised and the strain was placed on the bottom and sides of the structure. The timbers came into contact with the hull and as the screws were turned the vessel began to raise. We worked slowly because we did not know what was going to happen and we were underneath the hull. If it were to fall again we would be caught between it and the ground. We were very conscious of the massive object we were moving. In just a few minutes, seemingly without effort we had raised the hull high enough to allow placement of two larger type jacks along the chine and we no longer needed to be under the vessel to operate the jacks.

We slowly began to work each jack one click at a time. All the while tightening and backing off on the appropriate lines and come-a-longs. After a dozen clicks on the jacks, we realized there was no weight on the jacks, in fact there never had been.

On closer inspection we discovered the ropes and come-a-longs also had no strain on them. We also realized that while under the hull, using the screw jacks, the screws had turned without effort, indicating they were lifting nothing but themselves. We simply had been to preoccupied to notice.

We discovered that not only were the lever jacks not lifting any weight, but that they, nor the lifting pads on them were touching the hull. The hull was suspended an inch or so above the pads with nothing but Oklahoma air between the lifting pads and the edge of the hull. As we moved the levers the hull would raise, but the air space remained constant, and no weight was ever placed upon the jacks. We could not believe our eyes, but we also knew we had help, unseen to our eyes, but none the less help, raising the vessel that day.

We thought maybe somehow the vessel was in a state of balance, that was causing this phenomena, yet when we attempted to just raise it with our own strength it would not budge, it was just too heavy. Heavy and solid as a rock. Yet, when we moved the levers the vessel would raise,. It moved as if it was light as a feather, with the tools never touching the hull. We began to work quickly and excitedly and within minutes the hull rolled upright, seemingly on its own, and stood solidly and squarely upon the timbers under its keel.

We rapidly arranged braces under the bottom on both sides and stepped back looking at each other in total amazement. It was only eleven thirty am on a Saturday morning, Just in time for our weekly lunch at the little country cafe in Luther. We adjourned to our lunch, but it was a silent and thoughtful group that day.

You might expect we would be jumping around praising the Lord for what we had witnessed, but we were not. Each of us in his or her own way was face to face with our Lord and Master that morning, for we knew we had taken part with our own hands and backs in a miracle. We were also face to face as never before with the fact we were building a vessel which for some reason, as yet unknown to us, was truly blessed and special to the Lord.

The events of that morning, were never discussed afterward among ourselves, and until now have been kept private. They were and still are, to each of us, treasured jewels fastened securely within our spirits, adding substance to the faith we each have in our Lord Jesus. I hope my inadequate words have conveyed the enormity and importance of these events upon our lives to the reader. That one time, each of us in the presence of witnesses, were an active part of an act of God in concert with His hosts, as they gently and reverently lifted Maranatha, placing her once more upon her keel in readiness for completion.

No more work was done that day and the next being Sunday was our day of rest. Early Monday I began working to repair the damage and by noon all the repairs were made and it was as if the past few days had never happened. The tools including the table saw had not been damaged, other than a little mud, which was quickly removed. The only loss was two sheets of Formica we had purchased for counter tops. This had been stored under the hull and was crushed as the vessel fell on it. We considered this to be no great loss since Debbie and I had never liked the pattern. Therefore in the grand total all that was lost were a few hours of time and even these were not lost since we had been blessed to be participants and witnesses to the wonders of our God. Even though the enemy had tried to destroy the work our Lord had turned it into victory before our eyes.

View of vessel showing the Stern and Starboard side as seen a few short weeks later just prior to the hull being painted.

The second event took place as several small events over a period of several weeks which I have telescoped together for the many details are mundane with the outcome being the important detail.

———◦◦◦❧◦◦◦———

Everything these days must be licensed or registered. Boats, as most are aware, are usually registered with the state of residence of the owner. Corresponding numbers and decals are then applied to the bow declaring to the world the vessel has been duly taxed, it is really all about taxes you see. When all this is accomplished the vessel then is permitted to use whatever waterways may be found in which it might float.

Lesser known to those outside the seagoing professions, and the salt water yachting types, is a process of registration known as

"Documentation." In the United States this type of registration is issued by the federal government through the offices of the United States Coast Guard. Documentation carries with it certain legal benefits and status which makes it desirable for vessels intended to travel international waters.

Therefore, in September 1986 I began the process of obtaining documentation for the S/V Maranatha. After several weeks of phone calls and letters to various state and federal offices and Coast Guard offices around the country, I finally held the required forms in my hot little hands. They required only to be filled in and mailed to the Coast Guard station in St. Louis, Missouri, along with a fee of one hundred dollars.

I proceeded to fill in the blanks, without difficulty, until I came to one marked "Vessel H.I.N." I was stumped, what on God's green earth was a H.I.N.? I looked through all the bureaucratic mass of paper work I had collected on the subject of vessel documentation and with some effort discovered that H.I.N. was an acronym for hull identification number.

Well, I thought in my ignorance, that is easy since the Maranatha is the only one in the world like her, and according to the vision the first of many, so I entered the number "1" in this purely bureaucratic little box. Oh how foolish of me to think so simplistic an answer and reasoning would satisfy our blessed government bureaucracy. A week after mailing the papers along with the required fee, I received by return mail the fore mentioned documents with the required fee, and a nice letter from a nice lady named Yeoman Yevonne Smith. Yeoman Yevonne Smith informed me very nicely, that apparently I had misread or even misunderstood, for the number "1" most certainly was not a correct H.I.N. for my B.O.A.T. The H.I.N for any vessel documented by the United States Coast Guard and thereby the United States Government must consist of the M.I.N combined with the M.U.N. and the D.O.M., indeed something more lengthy than "1," even though the number "1" certainly was a very nice number.

Fortunately Yeoman Yevonne Smith had included a telephone number where she could be reached, and she stated she would be more than happy to assist me, in overcoming my all too simplistic approach to such important government procedures, and the apparent lack in understanding the proper respect, which should be directed towards important blocks, on the even more important government forms.

I called yeoman Yevonne Smith immediately and indeed found her to be most pleasant and delightful to talk to, although somewhat confused concerning our request for documentation. We just did not seem to fit into any of the appropriate government boxes. I soon, with her help, discovered the answer to the alphabet soup riddle contained in her letter, and indeed the cause for her dilemma, and my simplistic ignorance.

M.I.N. stands for "manufacturers identification number," while the M.U.N. is the "manufacturers hull number," and of course obvious to anyone except me, the D.O.M. is the "date of manufacture."

Soooo, the magic formula is MINMUNDOM=HIN. Simple right? Of course it is! Since the last two number sequences, letters, equal numbers, and may be mixed at will, are factors of manufacture, they offered little in the way of challenge. The very nice number "1" would be allowed if preceded by two zeros, I was simply delighted, I had grown rather attached to the very nice number "1."

The only item left for discovery was the elusive M.I.N. I told her Spirit Wind Ministries, was both the owner of the completed vessel and the materials which went into her construction, and that there were no leans or debtors involved. I also tentatively offered that Spirit Wind Ministries was also the manufacturer. That being the case would or could she, Yeoman Yevonne Smith, please assign a number which henceforth and forever would be our M.I.N.

Foolish me! She was aghast, such a request had never been made prior to this, and she knew not what to do. I was, however, put on hold while she spoke to a superior officer in an attempt to solve our dilemma.

She returned shortly and informed me I must write to the Commandants Office in Washington D.C., the very cradle of bureaucracy, with a formal request that Spirit Wind Ministries be assigned an official three digit manufacturers number. She also supplied the proper address, names and departments to be addressed. I thanked her kindly and hung up, relieved to at last have full and official knowledge of the meaning of the MINMUNDOM, and most importantly the ability to formulate the all important H.I.N., and the source for the information to accomplish this most important task.

I have had some fun here with all this and possibly at Ms. Smiths expense. I must set the record straight, for in my dealing with the Coast Guard and especially Ms. Smith, I was accorded the most courtesy and professionalism. Ms. Yeoman Yevonne Smith was delightful and I believe she enjoyed the humor of the situation as much as I.

The formal request was written and mailed to the Commandant U.S. Coast Guard, Office of Marine Safety, Washington D.C. I anxiously awaited the reply for one never knows what shadows lurk within the halls of Washington D.C. Anything can happen and often does to those who find themselves dealing directly with the offices of that awe-gust city.

Three weeks later on a Saturday, Bill brought the awaited reply, we used his shop address, since we would not have one when we departed. As he handed me the official envelope, I knew immediately what it should contain, but I did not know if we had been accepted or rejected for receipt of the required three digit number.

I opened the letter and began to read the official document enclosed. The first paragraph stated per our request we had been assigned an M.I.N. which was to become part of the H.I.N.'s assigned to vessels manufactured by Spirit Wind Ministries henceforth and forever. There was a space which appeared to simply be a space between paragraphs and the balance of the letter briefly explained the requirements and conditions required of holders of official M.I.N.'s.

Upon closer inspection it was obvious I was holding a form letter, one of several copies generated on a computer after certain information was inserted into its electronic brain. I still did not see our precious required three digit M.I.N.

Did someone forget to type it in, I wondered? I reread the letter slower this time, and as my eyes scanned across the space between paragraphs, there it was! It was a barley visible carbon impression, possibly because of the number of copies printed, but there it was, all but hidden neatly in the crease of the folded paper, our required three digit M.I.N.!

GOD

I let out a yell that woke up the neighbors and frightened Bill into dropping the grinder he held in his hands. I ran to him excitedly shoving the letter into his hands unable to speak, I was so excited. I grabbed the letter back from his hands as he finished reading it and raced into the trailer to show Debbie, I jumped for joy and shouted till I knew everyone thought I had finally gone round the bend without a return ticket. But, I held in my hand proof, my justification after all this time.

There on an official form letter, generated by a computer, generated in a completely random process, was a three digit designation naming for all the world to see, the manufacturer of the S/V Maranatha.

This letter stated in black and white that the official U.S. government through the offices of the Commandant U.S. Coast Guard recognized GOD to be the official builder of the S/V Maranatha.

That my friends is the significance of the manufacturers identification number. Even though on the paper work Spirit Wind Ministries is listed as manufacturer, anytime anyone reads the official number on the paper or on the two official bronze plates fastened to the hull of the vessel, the first thing they will read is GOD.

God is according to the U.S. government the builder of record and to this day it is so recorded in the halls of Washington D.C.!

The remainder of the paper work was filled out and along with the required fee promptly mailed to Yeoman Yevonne Smith. Two short weeks later we received S/V Maranatha's official papers, making her an officially documented vessel of the United States of America. Listed on these documents was her HIN consisting of her MINMUNDOM attesting to the world her manufacturer to be none other than GOD.

MOVING DAY

Christmas 1986 came and went and the new year took its place. Maranatha had stood serenely upon her hilltop decorated in colored lights for the holiday season. The traffic on the road was busy as all the locals drove by to view the completed vessel standing there in her fresh coat of paint, her turned spindle rails, and her bowsprit pointing eastward. She was an impressive sight as she dwarfed the trailer we lived in.

As a matter of fact, when we did finally move aboard, we found we had more living space than we did in the trailer. The exterior was basically complete, awaiting only the installation of the top hamper, sailor talk for masts, sails, cables and supporting hardware. Inside we were busy completing the living space to allow Debbie and I to live aboard as soon as we moved to the water.

The moving event was scheduled to take place the third week of January1987, just two short weeks away. The excitement and anticipation was strongly electric in the air as we hurried to complete the living quarters. This consisted mostly of electrical and plumbing installations. A large vessel requires more piping than a large home and everything must be operated by a battery of pumps, each dedicated to a specific function. Electricity is just as bad in its requirements, the salt water environment is extremely corrosive requiring everything to be painstakingly installed. Miniscule breaks in insulation can and will result in electrical problems in short order once exposed to salt air.

Painting and decorating were also being accomplished, but this was not a priority since Debbie and I could finish this after launching. I some times think sailors should be born with a paint brush in one hand and a mop in the other.

We had made all the necessary arrangements for the move with our friends Lippert Bros. Construction. They had made several trips out to the site to determine just what kind of equipment would be required to move the vessel. They were at first shocked at the size of the vessel, and I believe, just a little concerned about how they would accomplish the move.

However, in short order in true can-do spirit, the problems were solved and all was in readiness for the move. All that remained was securing permits and a routing from the state authorities. In Oklahoma this turned out to be the Oklahoma Corporation Commission. The commission regulates all traffic upon the highways in the state and sets the rates for license fees and also penalties. They have a reputation, so we found out, as one of the toughest in the nation. Enforcement officers of this commission carry unquestioned authority over all law enforcement agencies within the state of Oklahoma. In other words this is not an agency one ignores.

My contact at Lippert Bros. told me that as soon as I produced the necessary permits and routing they would move the Maranatha immediately. He gave me the phone numbers I should call and the process was underway. I was shocked to discover the permits and bond for the move would cost in excess of one thousand dollars. They could, however, be issued in time for our anticipated move date, providing I could somehow find the thousand dollars. Needless to say our funds did not have any amount remotely resembling that amount. Enter the never ending supply and planning of our Lord!

That evening was our study group meeting. Debbie and I arrived early and I mentioned to Frank, the leader of our group, I would like to submit the matter of the permit fee to the group for prayer. Frank smiled and said, "I work at the capitol. Let me see what I can find out first. Maybe I can help move things along and possibly reduce the fees a little."

"Great," I said, "we can use all the help we can get."

The matter was not mentioned again, we had a good group meeting and fellowship. We returned home refreshed and for the time being were unconcerned about funds for the permits. The next afternoon I was surprised to see Frank drive into the yard. I knew it was a work day for him and it was early in the afternoon. This being the first time he had visited, since our joining the group a few months earlier, we spent a good deal of time with the grand tour. Frank became more and more excited as he walked around the Maranatha and inspected the interior.

Bill who was present that day was strangely reserved. He had over the past few months become jealous of anyone who showed an interest in the project, or who took some of my time away from the work. I had grown accustomed to his moods and paid little attention to them. Finally after almost an hour Frank and I descended to the ground, it was then that Frank revealed his part in God's continuing miracle.

Frank, it turned out, had worked for the state of Oklahoma for a long time. He was currently ten years into his second career with the state. He had retired ten years earlier after twenty five years service in the Oklahoma State Highway Patrol. During his last ten years with the highway patrol he had served as the commandant, the number one man second only to the Governor. His current position was as the director of the Oklahoma State Corporation Commission. Again his authority being second only to that of the Governor of the state.

In fact in the hierarchy of state politics, his current office superseded all other state agencies. I had no idea of any of this until this moment and I stood there with my mouth open. This man, I simply knew as Frank and as a brother in Christ, was one of the most powerful men in the entire state of Oklahoma. Even more astounding was the news he brought after telling me about his position in state government.

He had, first thing, upon arrival at his office that morning contacted all of his department heads, instructing them to waive all permits and fees connected with our move, and to prepare a routing from the Luther hilltop to our launch point on Kerr-McGee lake south of Salisaw, Oklahoma. They also were as soon as possible, before noon, to provide that information to Lippert Bros. Construction Co. They were to request of Lippert a twenty four hour notice of the move, in order for the Corporation Commission escorts to arrange for the one hundred seventy eight mile move to the water.

Frank also upon his receiving the routing contacted the Oklahoma Highway Patrol, informing them of the proposed date and route, requesting them to keep the route clear, and to inform all local law enforcement agencies of the move. They were to inform them this was a special project of the Corporation Commission, and to stay clear, rendering only the requested assistance.

I looked at Frank without a thing to say, I was totally caught off guard by this turn of events. All I could say was a subdued "Thank You." He smiled as he got into his car, and said he was taking the afternoon off and was going home. He drove down the drive leaving me there rooted to the spot wondering at the provisions of our Lord, wondering what was next.

Bill descended to the ground a few minutes later wanting to know who Frank was and what he wanted. I explained it all to him and I cannot describe his reaction to this news, but it was not positive.

By the time Debbie arrived home the importance of the days events had sunk into my thick skull and I was dancing up and down waiting to tell her. She was just as amazed as I had been once the shock wore off. She and I rejoiced and praised the Lord together for His wonderful provision.

The next morning the foreman and the driver from Lippert Bros. arrived to make the final survey and determination of required equipment and labor. They were somewhat curious as they stated they did not know what strings had been pulled, but their boss had been contacted personally by the Supervisor in charge of permits at the state, telling him to let them know if they could be of any assistance in any way during this project. They just shook their heads as they approached the Maranatha with reverence. It seems the full blessing of the Corporation Commission had given these fellows a new respect for the task they had undertaken. They made their measurements, decisions, and departed saying they would be back at 7:00am to begin the loading.

That night it snowed!

It was not just the normal one inch Oklahoma duster but a major storm. The snow was still falling at noon the next day and accumulated to ten inches. To make matters worse prior to the snow there had been a typical Oklahoma ice storm leaving a thick covering of ice under the snow. The roads were impassable for days and once all the moisture melted the ground around the vessel was incapable of supporting the heavy equipment and trucks required to move the twenty four and a half ton Maranatha. The move was delayed indefinitely, though disappointing, it did allow us more time to complete the interior and work on the masts and spars which received their final shaping during this delay.

During this delay one more obstacle cropped up. A small independent telephone company along the route informed Lippert Bros. That they would not be allowed to lift any of this companies wires along the route. This service could only be preformed by company employees and with their equipment. The charge for this service would be one hundred fifty dollars per lift. It was estimated a minimum of twelve lifts would be required for our route making the charge an estimated one thousand eight hundred dollars. Once again a sum we did not currently have in our possession. I instructed Lippert Bros. to continue as planned, since the bill would not be submitted until after the move, and I felt assured the funds would be available to meet the obligation when required.

The weeks following the storm were busy, filled with completing as much work as possible prior to the move. Also included in all of this frantic activity was the small item of Debbie and I also moving our home. Maranatha was to be our new residence, therefore, we were also confronted with all the details of moving ones residence to another place, complicated by the fact the new residence floats with no permanent attachment to anything requiring essentially it to be self sufficient.

Our next door neighbor was convinced that the world should know of the happenings on our hilltop and had taken it upon herself to contact the news media in the area. The results being several interviews by newspaper reporters from both large and small newspapers and two television stations produced stories of our adventures. These were welcome but did complicate an all ready busy schedule.

Finally the day arrived when it was determined the ground was sufficiently stable to support the moving equipment. The necessary calls were made and at day break February 19, 1987, once again the month of Adar, was appointed as the time to begin the process of loading the S/V Maranatha onto the bed of a low-boy trailer for her move to Kerr-McGee lake south of Salisaw, Oklahoma. This lake is part of the Kerr-McCellan Navigation System. Oklahoma's gateway to the Gulf of Mexico.

I must admit I had not fully considered the requirements of men, materials, and equipment which would be required to move the Maranatha from her hilltop to her launching point some one hundred and eighty miles distant.

Debbie and I were somewhat overwhelmed as the men and materials began to arrive shortly after 8:00am that morning. We were told the cranes, plural, had departed Oklahoma City at day break and would arrive around noon. When questioned the Lippert foreman told us that they had decided their own crane was too small for the job so the Lippert's had contacted a friend of theirs who owned a crane rental company. They had told him of their problem and their involvement with our project, where upon he had volunteered the use of his largest tire equipped cranes, including the crews to operate them at no charge. Another small miracle!

The workmen busied themselves enlarging gates and making ready for the arrival of the cranes, Debbie and I could only stay out of the way answering questions when asked and providing drinks for the workers. Bill arrived shortly after the first trucks arrived, and once again seemed to be strangely affected by all the activity, but remained very busy himself gathering up tools and materials which would not make the journey, but were going to his shop for storage or his use.

Promptly at noon the first crane turned into our drive. I do not remember it's size but it was totally capable of lifting Maranatha by itself. When I asked why two such monsters were to be used, I was told, it was to insure absolute control and safety as the vessel was lifted. Also they felt there would be less strain placed upon the vessel as it was lifted. Indeed upon inspecting the job at hand the chief crane operator expressed concern the lifting straps would squeeze the structure and damage it when its weight was applied to the straps. I assured him there should not be any problems in that area as long as they could place the straps according to my directions.

View of vessel showing the crane on the Starboard side lifting a compressor off the deck just prior to the lifting straps being put in place. Part of the old trailer house shows on the right side of the picture. The men in the picture are Lippert Brothers Construction Company employees.

The second crane rolled into the yard a few minutes later and behind it the news crew from channel five in Oklahoma City. Following that a string of vehicles filled with more workers and officials from Lippert Bros. and the crane company, carrying their cameras, with which to document this event for their company records.

Debbie and I were kept very busy for the next couple of hours, playing host to these benefactors, and answering the news crews questions. Bill, of a sudden was not in the center of things, although we did not intentionally ignore him. It just happened that the events of the next two days did not revolve around or involve him. With hind sight I see now that this added to the beginnings of our troubles with our beloved friend.

While we were thus engaged the construction and crane crews made their preparations, signaling me when they were ready. Everyone held their breath as the slings were placed and the crane operators took up the slack in the cables and slings and the vessel began to lift off her supporting cradle. Ever so slowly they inched the cables in their big machines upward and the straps became tight, the without a sound daylight appeared under the keel. Then all movement was stopped while I got underneath to paint the bottom of the keel with anti-fouling paint and to inspect for any sign of damage. There was none.

The vessel then raised a few inches higher and the low-boy trailer was backed underneath. Then just as slowly as it was raised it was gently lowered onto the truck until the keel came to rest on timbers placed at intervals along the trailer. The cranes kept their supporting straps tight to support the vessel until the workmen could construct the cradle which would support the vessel during transport. Enough of the cradle was completed by 5:00pm to support the hull on the trailer and the two cranes were released to start their way back to Oklahoma City.

Maranatha being placed on the trailer by the cranes.
Again the men in the picture are Lippert Brothers employees.

Prior to their departure the lead crane operator told me he had never lifted a stronger object. He stated he had expected all types of movement and accompanying squeaks and squawks as they lifted the hull and its full weight registered on the scales of the cranes. He was totally surprised when there were no sounds or motion as the hull was lifted. I smiled remembering the day not so long before when we had lifted the hull back to its resting place after the surprise thunderstorm.

With the departure of the cranes all work ceased for the day and the foreman informed me they would be back the next morning to finish the cradle and preparations for the road. Just prior to departure one of the cranes had loaded the masts onto another trailer, so as the last of the workmen drove down the drive we went inside to watch ourselves on the six o'clock news, considering the day well spent.

Bill seemed to be over his mood and departed shortly after we watched the Maranatha being lifted into the air as news woman Jane Bryant tried to tell the story of the past two years in ninety seconds to her television audience.

The next day the workers returned and completed the cradle to their satisfaction by noon. The cradle they fashioned was strong enough to carry the weight of five Maranatha's. It was also no rough piece of carpentry, the men had taken great pains to fashion, from heavy timber, a thing of beauty. They had fashioned it as a finished object leaving no rough edges or projections. As with everyone the Lord had allowed to touch and work with his vessel they seemed to know the work they were doing was special and took great care to do the work with skill and pride. They knew full well that in just two days the cradle would be dismantled as the vessel was unloaded at Applegate Cove Marina, yet they built it as if it would stand forever.

The last day in Luther was hectic for us, as we worked late loading supplies, tools, and equipment, as well as personal items into the boat. I was distracted many times by visitors and friends who as a result of the publicity had decided to renew our friendship prior to our departure. The longest distraction was by a reporter from the Daily Oklahoman who had been sent by his editor to find out what all the fuss was about.

Bill was very upset by the amount of time I spent talking to this man, as a result he and I spoke our first harsh words, as he confronted me for not doing my part of the work. Somehow along the way I had begun to work for him, instead of him working for the ministry. Bill's attitude gradually began to deteriorate as we began the transition to water and the Lord began to bring others and their assets to the ministry. It was a very long time before I realized why.

It seems that somewhere a long the way, the building of the Maranatha, became Bill's personal project and he began to look upon her as his personal property. True he had contributed a very large amount of money and his time, but somewhere along the way the ministry became his, not God's, and I was taking the ship away from him. I had difficulty understanding the change in him, partly because I was very busy with the details involved in bring this phase of the project to it's conclusion. The events taking place were nothing which had not been planned and talked of for months and years prior to Bill joining the project. Unfortunately for our relationship I simply was not sensitive enough for his needs.

So on the last evening Maranatha was to spend on the red Oklahoma hilltop southeast of Luther, Oklahoma, unknown to Debbie and I, there was discord in the camp. As Debbie and I celebrated our last evening at the trailer in Luther, which had been our home for just over a year, we were unaware of the turmoil that was building in Bill's heart as he knew the Maranatha was leaving her hilltop in central Oklahoma without him.

WATER AT LAST

Shortly before dawn the morning of February 21,1987 the Lippert Bros. driver arrived to inspect his cargo. Frank arrived to act as escort to the first state highway, where his enforcement officers would meet us, one would be in front and one would be in the rear of our column, driving their official Oklahoma state patrol cars to act as escorts. Bill arrived before daybreak to witness the departure, but stated he would not make the trip with us.

After a brief prayer we all went to our respective vehicles, I was to ride with the driver of the truck and Debbie was to ride with Frank.

I cannot even after all these years find words to adequately describe my feelings that morning as the truck started up and the Maranatha began its journey to water. True there would be several months work before she was complete, however, this morning was the day for which Debbie and I had worked and suffered for several years of our lives. The day which together Debbie and I had for almost two and a half years sacrificed everything we had to see come to pass.

As the truck turned from the drive onto the road and turned east into the sunrise I remembered another sunrise two years and hundreds of miles from the hilltop in central Oklahoma. I heard once more the promise made to me that morning in the islands and I was at peace, knowing the Lord was with us, as I turned my attention to the task of the day.

Little known to those outside the state of Oklahoma, and to many who live within the state, is that tucked within the hills and trees of eastern Oklahoma, is a major shipping avenue connecting Tulsa directly with all the oceans of the world via the Mississippi river and the gulf of Mexico. This is made possible by a series of locks and dams on the Arkansas river westward from the Mississippi river, five hundred plus miles to the Port of Catoosa just east of Tulsa, Oklahoma. Known as the Kerr-McCellan Arkansas River Navigation System. Thousand of tons of agricultural products, coal, and finished goods are shipped to ports around the world via this waterway each year. Also tons of trade goods make their way upstream as well each year, making this waterway, a major economic factor in Oklahoma and Arkansas. It was to this waterway we were headed, it was our gateway to the sea, and specifically the islands of the Caribbean.

We were on our way to Applegate Cove Marina approximately five miles upstream from lock and dam #15 of this system. The marina is located approximately twenty miles south of Salisaw, Oklahoma. Our route was to zigzag east southeast across the state for one hundred seventy eight miles. We were using secondary highways, which had no bridges or overpasses, which we would be required to pass under.

The Maranatha measured slightly over eighteen feet from the ground to the highest point above ground, much to high to transit most highway overpasses. We needed to be on constant lookout for wires crossing the roadway. We had two Lippert Bros. pickup trucks, one in front and one in the rear, who would stop and raise the wires for the vessel to pass under safely. Then we would speed up until the next wires would be reached. Needless to say this caused progress to be very slow and time consuming.

The first town of any size we were to pass through was Meeker, Oklahoma. This was also the home of the telephone company which insisted upon raising their own wires at the rate of one hundred and fifty dollars per wire. We were met at the outskirts of town by the phone company representatives wringing their hands at the prospect of the easy cash coming their way. You could see their faces fall as they saw our escort of Corporation Commission Enforcement Officers.

**Maranatha as she passing through Meeker Oklahoma
dodging traffic lights. I remember this as being a real nail biter.**

A local policeman who had not gotten the word, rushed up with lights flashing, ticket book in hand, with a gleam in his eye at the prospect of fine dollars clinking into the till. He was immediately cut off by two state vehicles, a few low voiced words were exchanged, resulting in him backing up his squad car and racing to the head of our column to assure our safe passage.

Upon seeing this, the phone company representatives issued instructions to their crews, who then raced ahead raising telephone and power lines which happened to be in our path. The telephone representatives spoke briefly to one of the enforcement officers and disappeared. I learned at the end of our trip, they had informed him, they had decided to waive the fees for passing through their territory. It seems they were very impressed with our status in the eyes of the State of Oklahoma. I also was told that the Corporation Commission also regulates the telephone companies in Oklahoma. Nothing was said to them and we were prepared to pay the fees upon receipt of a bill, however, the Lord had other ideas and their greed melted before the force of the authority the Lord displayed before them.

The balance of the day was uneventful as we worked our way through central Oklahoma on our way east. The Maranatha caused much excitement as she passed through the small Oklahoma towns along the way. People would stop whatever they were doing to watch her pass. On several occasions we were able to briefly tell her story as witness to the people along the way.

Noon time found us in Eufala, Oklahoma and we stopped for lunch. The escorts, drivers and Lippert employees along with Frank, Debbie and I almost filled the restaurant and there were many questions about the large boat parked in their lot. The balance of the afternoon was more of the same small towns, lifting wires, moving slowly but surely toward our destination.

About five pm, we were passing through the town of Snyder, Oklahoma. Coming as we did from the area of the largest city in the state, we did not even consider this small town would have a rush hour. Yet as we entered the western edge of the small town, we discovered that even in rural Oklahoma a small town can have a rush hour. We complicated things immensely, however, our escorts had contacted the local authorities and they controlled traffic allowing us to pass through as quickly possible.

We stopped on the eastern side of town to thank the local Chief of Police for his help which he accepted graciously. He was also in awe of our cargo and it's escort. During our brief conversation he told us that during our brief passage through his town, a distance of about two miles, there had been no less then six rear end collisions, caused by people staring opened mouthed at the Maranatha as she passed. There had been no injuries and little or no property damage, however, which pleased us very much. The Lord had not only taken us and His vessel safely through the town, but He also had protected those along the way who had become awe struck with her size and beauty.

Shortly after passing through this small town darkness stopped our progress for the day. We pulled of the road on a wide shoulder in front of a farm house just fifty miles from our destination. I decided to stay with the Maranatha for the night, and as Frank and Debbie went to find a restaurant, I climbed up onto the deck and made my way below for an inspection.

I found as I entered the cabins that nothing was out of place. Not one thing stored inside had moved. It was as if the vessel had not traveled over one hundred miles from her birth place, while at times being bounced heavily by the back country highways. I returned to the deck and waited for Debbie and Frank to return with my evening meal.

While I waited a lady from the farm house rather timidly approached and said hello. After brief introductions I told her Maranatha's story as we waited for Debbie and Frank to return. They arrived shortly and I said goodbye to them. Debbie was going back to finish our packing the next day and Frank had to put in a day at his office. He assured me his officers would meet us in the morning to finish escorting us to the marina. It was very dark and cold as they departed, but I once again descended into Maranatha, ate my dinner and snuggled down warmly for a good nights rest.

You might think such an attraction, as was presented by the Maranatha parked along that dark country highway, might attract those bent on doing no-good. Early in the evening I did hear a few cars slow as they passed, but none came to a halt. Maranatha and I passed a restful night with none attempting to cause us harm.

Within minutes of my coming on deck the next morning the family from the farm house brought me coffee and breakfast, for which I was most grateful. I had hardly finished it when the Lippert crew arrived. They quickly had the truck started and I said goodbye to my friends from the house, climbed into the truck and we were on our way once more.

Frank's officers met us within minutes, falling in at the front and rear of the column. As it happened there were no more low wires or towns to pass until we reached the state park area which housed Applegate Cove Marina. So we made the last fifty miles of our journey in just over an hour. We arrived at the marina at approximately 8:30am on the morning of February 22,1987, two years to the day from the evening the prayer meeting was held in an empty warehouse in south Oklahoma City, and the first nails were driven into the lofting floor. The official beginning of the physical presence of the Schooner Maranatha.

Preparations were quickly made and a large portable boat lift was moved into place, the cradle was partially demolished and the Maranatha was lifted clear of the truck and the remains of the cradle and moved very tenderly out over the water of Kerr lake. I held my breath and prayed very quietly, I did not know what else to do. The importance of the moment was not lost upon me, but by that time I had little emotion remaining.

Slowly, ever so slowly, the hull was lowered towards the water. I had no doubt she would float, but still I was filled with apprehension. Finally the keel kissed the surface of the water then disappeared beneath it with the hull resting on the water, floating lightly between the straps just as she should.

A cheer was raised by the small crowd of people gathered to witness the launching. The crew of Lippert Bros., the Corporation Commission Officers, the owners and employees of the marina, myself and all the angels who for months had helped me in the construction of the vessel. I felt their presence and in the corner of my eye I could see them cheering and dancing for joy as their beloved Maranatha touched water at last.

APPLEGATE COVE GATEWAY
TO THE WORLD

The first few days at the marina were busy ones. The Lippert driver had made a quick round trip the day of the launching while I had remained with the vessel. He returned in the early afternoon with the masts, spars and the dingy, "Honey."

Immediately upon off loading with me joining him we returned to Oklahoma City, that evening, leaving Maranatha secure in her slip at the marina. That evening and the next day, with the help of Bill, Frank and two or three others, we finished our move from the hill top near Luther. Many of our possessions were put in storage at Bill's shop, while those we could use were loaded into our car.

We spent that night in Edmond, Oklahoma, planning to drive to Salisaw and the Maranatha after church the next morning. This we did, arriving at the marina in the late afternoon. Debbie and I felt good about the move, and somewhat excited about being by ourselves for a little while, it seemed that for months we had seen little of each other, since there had usually been someone around when we did see each other.

The first few days were blessed and we simply took them as they came, allowing ourselves to rest, and become accustomed to living on board the vessel. We busied ourselves, stowing away our belongings and converting the Maranatha into the home she was to be for us for the next several years.

Our vacation was short lived as Bill arrived unannounced early one morning, suddenly appearing through the forward companionway as

Debbie and I were finishing breakfast. We were startled for he had boarded quietly and we were unaware of his presence until he suddenly appeared.

He was very brusque, wanting to know what I had been doing since we had arrived. He seemed unhappy with my answers, I for some reason found myself on the defensive, as though I was being confronted by an irate employer. I was now fully aware that Bill considered the Maranatha to be his and was fighting a real battle with himself over no longer having control over the situation.

However, from that day until we parted in June he continued to work on the ship, as he called it, helping with final details. Yet, he grew more and more combative, and our friendship deteriorated gradually from that point. Bill wanted total control over the project, and I as the appointed leader could not give it to him, for I was responsible for the success of the project. Though he would not admit it he was not the only contributor to the mission and he was not charged with its success or failure.

The work, however, continued and a week before Easter 1987 we stepped the masts with hardware and installed the gaffs and booms. For the first time with her top-hamper installed Maranatha became the tall ship which was her destiny. The engine was running and was daily presenting us with one problem after another consuming time away from other projects. This was to be the pattern almost daily for the next two years as that little Opel/ Isuzu engine made itself the bane of our existence. The refrigeration and freezer system was working well and at the time was my only satisfaction for putting up with the engine. I also at the time had no idea the engine and its problems would never be resolved. Indeed had I then known these things, I would have instantly converted the engine into a large but ungainly anchor.

All other preparations for departure were going well as the tackle was manufactured for sail handling and our anchoring equipment was installed. The interior was virtually complete and other than one last major item we were ready to begin our journey.

This last item, however, was very major, it was our sails. I had determined very early that a suit of sails sewn by any of the sail manufacturers in the country would be out of the question financially. So we had decided to sew our own. We had decided to purchase sail kits designed for our rig from a company who specialized in providing build your own kits to the sailing public. Yet, even with this cost saving effort the cost of Maranatha's sails would be over two thousand dollars. Funds which as usual we did not have.

With the approach of Easter, Debbie and I both felt the need to hold services on board the Maranatha. We obtained permission from the owners of the marina, then prepared and distributed hand written invitations to each boat in the marina. There were several large boats which always had owners in residence during the weekends. We had made acquaintance with one or two, but truthfully had no idea if anyone would attend our service.

We had decided to hold a Eucharist service and had made our plans accordingly. Easter morning arrived, it was a beautiful spring morning. We had set the time of the service at 10:00 am which should, we thought, allow everyone time to make the service without being rushed or having to rise early, after all they were at the marina for relaxation.

We were ready hours early, pumped with anticipation, not knowing how our invitations had been received. We spent the time checking and rechecking our preparations, cautiously looking down the pier for signs of any one approaching in our direction.

A few minutes before ten I was below when I heard Debbie say, "Oh Lord look at them come." I popped my head up through the hatch to see people headed our way, coming down our pier from every direction and occupied boat in the marina. We were over joyed, the response was better than we had dared hope, it was a pretty good start to the ministry life of the Maranatha!

We welcomed our guests abroad the Maranatha, and spent the first thirty minutes or so showing those who wished to see her, through the vessel. The service we conducted that morning was brief. We spent most of the time singing. The brief homily reinforced the significance of the day and the Eucharist of which we were to partake. The Elements we offered to all and none refused. Their names were all entered into the log of the Maranatha, recording the first Holy service held on board. We were thanked warmly by those who attended for the relaxed and casual service. They told us they were grateful for the reminder, that even in their recreation, they should take time to honor the Lord and remember His sacrifice for us.

A few days after Easter we decided to try and raise funds for the sails with a sale and auction. It would be held and run by the home study group we had been part of the past few months. Everyone had something to contribute and a few days prior to the sale Debbie returned to Oklahoma City to sort through our belongings in storage for items to contribute. She remained in Oklahoma City until after the sale and returned with the news that just under three thousand dollars had been raised by the sale. Mostly through the sale of our own personal property. The only thing we had left were a few books, papers and pictures, and the few things we had brought with us to the boat.

Our quest for the funds for the sails had been answered, the Lord had provided and we rejoiced. I called Bill and Frank and gave the instructions to pay for the sail kits, and called the sail company and ordered the sails. The cost of the full set of one thousand eight hundred fifty feet of canvas came to Two thousand and Fifty dollars. This left us with a remainder of around eight hundred dollars. We had done well with the sale and looked forward to the arrival of the sail material. Then the completion of the Maranatha and all her necessaries would be accomplished and we could start our journeys.

Bill arrived the next morning and much to my consternation I was told the money had not been forwarded for the sails. It seems he and Frank, mostly Bill, had decided I was spending too much money on the sails and he, Bill, was not going to release the money until he got his way or was convinced there was no cheaper route to obtaining the sails for the vessel. I will not describe the conversation we had that day, but by the time Bill left us that afternoon a cashiers check was on its way to the sail makers. Yet, Bill was determined I had made the final error, as he departed for home.

A week later the sail material arrived at Bill's shop in Oklahoma City. Plans were made for us to return to the city in order to make the sails. We needed a large flat surface in order to loft the patterns and cut the material. The sail cloth came in thirty two inch wide bolts of cloth. From these the many panels required would be cut to length as they were rolled out upon the patterns lofted on the large flat surface.

Bill and I had discussed the need for a large space with a clean flat surface at length. Finally he had approached his pastor asking for the use of the church gymnasium for a week. This he informed me was welcomed. All we had to do was tell them when we wished to do the work. We decided to do the work during the Memorial Day week starting on Wednesday, planning to be finished on Saturday, returning to Salisaw and the Maranatha on Sunday after church with the completed sails. Bill flew down on Tuesday morning and Debbie went to pick him up at the small airport a few miles north of the lake.

Our plan was to finish some last minute details that day and fly back to the city that evening. Without so much as a hello Bill thrust a small piece of fabric into Debbie's hand and angrily said, "This isn't the right stuff. Judd says this will never work. It's too stiff and will never be right. I told Ken he was making a mistake, and now I can say I told him so, he's wasted all that money and still won't have any sails for the ship. He just should have listened to me and done what I wanted. Now the whole sail thing will have to be done over."

Debbie, of course was instantly on the defensive, for no one was going to talk to her in that manner, and certainly was not going to talk about me in that fashion either.

"Well Bill," she shot back, "I wouldn't know sail cloth if it jumped up and kicked me in the face. As for Judd, he's a very nice man, but he's an upholster, not a sail maker, and even I know there's a world of difference. I also think that at this late date if your going to question Ken's judgment you should do so to his face instead of going to someone outside the ministry. Further don't jump on me because you think you have something to be upset about, Ken should have been consulted before you even opened the packages. Now are you ready to go to the lake?"

The few miles back to the lake, where I waited unknowingly, provided a very chilly ride for Bill that Oklahoma spring morning. In fact if not for my wife's ability to walk in grace almost effortlessly, Bill would have found himself standing there in his indignation all by his lonesome, as we say in Oklahoma.

Nothing was said about their discussion when they arrived. Bill handed me the small scrap of cloth and immediately went to work. I looked at the cloth and was glad to see it was exactly what I had ordered. Debbie then told me of her altercation at the airport. I was disturbed by this news, but passed it off, because the cloth was the proper material. Yet, I was unsure about Bill's reaction and continued bitterness over the funds spent for the sail materials.

Nothing further was said to me until later that day on the way to the airport when Bill stated, "I showed Judd that piece of cloth I gave you and he says it's not the right thing. It's too stiff and won't bend properly."

"Well Judd's a nice man, I couldn't resist throwing Debbie's words back at him, "but in this case he's wrong. Because the material is correct, in fact it is heavier than I'd expected which is great as far as I'm concerned. The cloth is heavy and stiff so it will stand up to years of use and the heavy pressures involved in providing power for a vessel the size of Maranatha. I am very pleased with what I've seen so far and am anxious to see the patterns and the rest of the kits."

"Well," Bill shot back, "it's not kits, it's just two very large rolls of this stuff and a couple of small boxes." He was just not going to give up. The next morning we arrived at his shop and as I had expected the materials shipped were exactly as I had ordered and anticipated. They did, however, appear to represent a lot more work than I had expected.

The morning was passing quickly, and I mentioned to Bill a few times, our need to move to the church gymnasium to begin the assembly of the sails. He did not respond and did nothing to start that process. Finally I asked him point blank if I should call the church to let them know we were on the way. His reply was to finally call them. I was flabbergasted to learn that he had not called them to make the arrangements and further flabbergasted to learn that they had refused us the use their gymnasium. I was very upset and concerned about this latest development in our relationship with Bill.

"Well I Guess," Bill stated, "I'll take you two back to the ship, since you can't make the sails, there's no reason to stay here." He seemed pleased with himself and I became very angry. "Not until I make a phone call," I stated. I picked up the phone book and quickly found the number I needed, and I dialed the number. I quickly explained the situation to the person who answered, waited a few moments as another person was consulted, I got my answer, thanked the person on the other end of the line and hung up. Bill stood there all the while with a puzzled look on his face.

Well," I said, "We are not going back to the lake yet! Let's load everything up and take it to Capital Hill United Methodist Church. We have unlimited use of their facilities for the construction of the sails."

Bill's mouth hit the floor. "Right now, just like that?" he asked.

"Just like that." I said.

"Is your friend going to meet us there?" He asked.

"No, Lowrie and Judy are out of town and won't be back until next week. The secretary asked one of the board members and he was overjoyed with the opportunity to help. They've even offered people to help us with the work if we need them." I told him.

Nothing more was said, but I realized he was not thrilled with the turn of events. I know now, that he had finally realized, he did not have the control he thought he did, or the control he wished to have.

The next few days were very busy as Debbie and I along with the people of the Methodist Congregation converted their gymnasium into a sail loft. Everyone was having a wonderful time, except Bill, for him nothing seemed right. He was one very frustrated man.

The work was interrupted Saturday morning, when we learned from the marina owners, that a group of people had moved on to the Maranatha and set up for the weekend. We were shell socked, none of the names we were given meant a thing to us, and attempts by the managers to dislodge them had proved futile. Finally, after several phone conversations, we learned their identity and the marina managers convinced them to leave or face arrest as trespassers.

The intruders were members of Bill's church, from of all things, the adult singles group. One of the men had been instrumental in helping us obtain the masts and spars, or the poles from which they were constructed, from his employers. How this translated into the minds of these people as the right to use the vessel at their discretion, without asking for permission, or without any consideration for the fact that we had the Maranatha locked up tight, I will never understand. They even had to break a lock and hasp to gain entry and avail themselves of Maranatha's hospitality.

Never mind that this was our home and seven of the eight people had never met us. Yet these brothers and sisters were very upset and extremely rude to those at the marina who were doing their best to do their jobs and protect the vessel left in their care. They very defiantly declared to the marina staff, "This boat is a Christian Missionary boat and as Christians we have every right to be here! We're not leaving 'til we are ready!" They finally did leave, however, about thirty minutes before we arrived from Oklahoma City to confront them.

I shudder at the witness they left behind with the marina folks. We had worked very hard to instill a favorable witness with the folks at the marina. Now this witness, was severely damaged by a group of thoughtless spoiled and pampered baby Christians.

Christian church people God love 'em! I know God does, but sometimes I find it extremely difficult!

I have never understood the belief by some Christians, that if it is connected with the church or a ministry, it becomes public Christian property and may be used as they wish, even if they themselves have no involvement in that particular ministry. I suppose this belief fits closely with "church cheap", along with the fact every large group has its share of hoodlums. Even, I am sorry to say, the Christian community.

We later learned that this group had approached Bill, something he never admitted, and asked if they could spend the Memorial Day weekend on board Maranatha as a group outing. Yet no one had bothered to inform or ask Debbie or I. Neither did anyone consider, that the Maranatha was our home, and we would not be home at the time of their visit.

After all settled down I suppose the fault rested squarely with Bill. The members of the group, however, hold blame as they should have made certain before they invaded our home unannounced. They also hold even more blame for the witness and bad taste they created for "Christians" with the people with whom they came into contact while enjoying their weekend at the lake.

I returned to Oklahoma City with Bill, while Debbie remained behind to rectify the mess left by our guests. None the less and among continued protest that they would never work, a few days later I returned to the Maranatha with the sails. There remained only a few details which required hand stitching and this could be done on board easily. Over the next few days the sails were carefully finished and fitted to their spars. Bill arrived on Thursday with his wife and another couple and was very displeased when he discovered the sail installation was not complete. There still remained the grommets for the Fore and Main sail installation. These consisted of nothing more than short lengths of small line which was to be passed through the eyes in the sail and knotted around the gaff or boom for each sail. Not a particularly technical job, but one which took considerable time to accomplish properly, due to the size of Maranatha's sails.

Over my objections Bill, hurriedly began cutting short lengths of line, paying little attention to their length. He was insistent that this task had to be accomplished with all haste and his attitude was one of barely concealed anger. A very tense afternoon was had by all, yet, an hour or so before sundown this task had been finished. Bill immediately began to make preparations to take the boat out on to the lake.

"What are you doing?" I asked.

"I've got to go back to the city and I'm going to sail this boat before I go home tonight!" He declared.

"No your not." I stated flatly.

"And just why not?" He asked. His eyes and voice daring me to stop him.

"Well first of all you do not know how to sail." I said.

"Well you do!" he interrupted, "Don't you think I deserve to see this ship under sail, after all I've done?"

I was taken by surprise by his outburst and took several moments to gather my thoughts, while he glared at me accusingly.

"Bill, of course you deserve to sail this vessel, if anyone does. But, this is not the proper time to do it. We have just a short time before dark, that is not the time to take an untried vessel on her maiden sail. If something happened, darkness is not the condition under which you need to be trying to figure out a new system as complicated as this. I'm the only one here who has even the remotest idea what all these lines are for, and night time is not the time I choose to give instructions. Not to mention we have not yet hoisted the fore and main to see if they've been laced on correctly, and even if they fit. I'm extremely sorry your so upset, but the Maranatha is not going out on the lake tonight nor anytime until I am satisfied the rigging has been properly installed and works as required for proper and safe handling of the vessel." I firmly informed him.

"Let's go home." He said to the others with him as he abruptly turned and stepped from the vessel. He did not look back, as he hurried down the dock, leaving the others behind. Debbie and I were left in a state of uncertainty and very disturbed by this turn of events. We did not dwell on it, however, and committed the entire affair to prayer.

Over the next few days the whole thing blew over, the sails were tested and checked, ending with the Maranatha being given, her maiden sail, early one morning the first week of June 1987. Bill was not present, and he was never to witness the beauty of Maranatha under sail with a fresh breeze in her teeth.

On Monday the 6th of June, 1987 at 6am the Maranatha slipped her moorings at Applegate Cove marina. With a company of eight souls on board she moved onto Kerr Lake. She pointed her bow down river saying goodbye forever to her birth place of Oklahoma. Her bow rose slightly in the moderate breeze as she looked forward to the rivers, gulfs, and oceans of the world.

This picture was taken from another boat by friends who were escorting us a short distance down river as we were leaving Oklahoma on the beginning of our journey.

EPILOGUE

The voyage of the MS/V Maranatha has ended, at least her voyage here on this world. Her voyage ended on a cold stormy evening, February 24, 1990, the month of Adar, off the north coast of Florida. I firmly believe I will once more stand her decks, as she sails the Crystal Sea, in the continuing service of our Lord.

The visions continue to this day, as I complete this writing in the year 2015. I sometimes wonder why, as it seems there will not again be a time for Debbie and I to do the work involved, in all that I am given to see. Yet, I know it will not be accomplished without me. I have come to believe the work is work that will be accomplished in the millennium to come.

Debbie and I now live in Warm Springs, Georgia. After the loss of the Maranatha, Debbie had a successful career with a major hotel chain and because of her position we moved to Georgia.

I put my Captains license to work and spent several years as a ships captain in the Gulf of Mexico. I eventually retired from the sea, or "put the oar over my shoulder and walked inland until someone asked me what that thing on my shoulder was," as the old sailors used to say.

I went back to school and received my Master of Divinity degree from Candler School of Theology, Emory University, Atlanta Georgia and a Doctor of Ministry from The King's Seminary in Van Nuys, California. I served for a number of years as pastor for several United Methodist Churches in north Georgia. Debbie now serves as Pastor for a rural United Methodist church close to Pine Mountain, Georgia. We both are now active with the Christian Motorcyclists Association and I spend my ministerial time now among the motorcycle community.

I do not know what the future holds for us, yet, I get a small glimmer now and then through some of the events the Lord takes us through. The desire to serve Him and do the work he has called us to, is as strong as ever, even though it appears it is not to be. Every time I hear a mission ask for help, sometimes pleading for help. I always say "I'll go Lord, pick me!" yet, He never does. Instead I am filled once more with the visions and the tasks yet to be accomplished, but never the answers to the questions of How, Where, When, and with What.

I wonder sometimes if I am simply the victim of auditory delusions, as my psychologists friends Tom and Stephanie would and have said, that all this is nothing more than the ramblings of a mind on the fringe. The difficulty being several others lived through the same delusions and suffered, in some cases, right along side of me. When I wonder, I am always brought back to the day so long ago when the Lord came to me and stood at the foot of my hospital bed. I hear again the words He spoke and I am immersed in his cool, comforting sweet voice. I know again it is real and even with all my doubts, my inequities, and my ineptitude, He, the Lord God of the universe chose me to accomplish this task and I have not yet been released from the call.

There have been those over the years who have accused me of being a fraud and a fake. They have pointed their fingers with righteous indignation, saying vigorously, that I have simply invented all this to justify taking money and offerings in order to fund the building of a boat. I have done this they say, so that I would not have to work for a living, and other things not so kind. My answer to them is the life we led, and the hardships we endured in an effort to follow the Lord. No one would chose such a life. If I was to invent something like this, I would chose something much less stressful and demanding, in order to live the comfortable life proposed in the accusations.

Some have used our difficulties as the proof of their accusations. The most recent and damning of all, "I know one thing for sure, the Lord does not have a vessel like the Maranatha built only to sink it!

Wasting all that money! It is always the money. "How do you explain that, if you are really sent from the Lord?"

I had no answer for them and for a very long time this one thing ate at my soul. Every night for four years after her loss, I relived that event in my dreams, attempting to discover the error I had made which had cost Maranatha her life. I spent countless hours reliving her building and every event leading up to her death, searching for an answer to why she had to die. This I lived with everyday for four years after her loss, and even to this day this event plagues my thoughts and memories.

Finally, on the morning of the forth anniversary of her loss, I was at sea alone on the bridge of the "MV Candy Cane," a vessel I captained while working in the Gulf of Mexico, off the south west coast of Louisiana. My mind was full of memories of Maranatha, such sweet memories. I was heart broken for I truly loved her, I began to sing praise songs to the Lord thanking Him for her and my memories. For close to five hours the Lord and I sang her praises and His as well. We had a very good time of praise and worship and that morning I finally buried the Maranatha. The dreams stopped and I no longer have the guilt I felt over her loss. I did not receive an answer to the questions, yet, I was set free of her burden. Something I believe I was never meant to carry in the first place.

I believe now I have the answer. I wish I could say I found it myself through study and prayer, and maybe it was all that which brought the answer to me, some day I believe I will know. The answer was given to me one morning as I drove across Alabama and Mississippi on my way to two more weeks at sea. It was my habit to listen to Christian radio on my drive to work. The nine to ten hours spent that way gave me the spiritual strength to face the foulness that can sometimes come as part of a sailors life among other sailors. The expression "cuss like a sailor" was coined for a reason.

On this particular trip as I listened to the speaker, whom I do not know, I heard the answer to all the accusations leveled at me for years. As it most always is, it had been resting there between the pages of the scriptures all the while. So if the reader will allow me a small amount of plagiarism I will attempt to set forth the answer.

First of all the Lord did not destroy the Maranatha! He loves her as much as I. She belongs to Him and always has. He says in the scriptures, "What has been given to me I will not lose." So how could He destroy the vessel? He could not! Also He did not cause the horse to kick me, nearly destroying my life so long ago. He is not the author of pain and since I was dedicated to Him, He has promised to protect and provide for me. Therefore, how could He have caused my trauma? He could not! All the other trials we went through, some of which I have written here and you have read, how could He have been the author of these things? He could not! He has promised and for Him to go against His promise would make Him to be false and a lair. May it never be!

So you ask what is the answer? Simply this, the enemies of the Lord Jesus know no limits to the hate they hold for Him. They were not satisfied with Calvary! That needs repeating, they were not satisfied with Calvary! Our Lord, though He suffered beyond our knowing, in their minds, He did not suffer enough. They believe that Calvary was actually a defeat rather than a victory. They know they were defeated by the cross they vilify and that their time is limited. Our Lord has the victory and through Him we have it also.

These enemies still look for ways to inflict pain and destruction upon Him, our Lord Jesus, and since he lives in this world through us, they inflict that pain and suffering upon us at every opportunity. The Apostle Paul speaks of this when he states, "I bare in my body the marks of Jesus." These are not the literal scars of the cross, but those caused from the wounds inflicted by the enemies of Jesus.

These were inflicted in an effort to cause, through Paul, more pain and suffering for the Lord. Therefore, by substitution Paul bore the wounds meant for our Lord. Sufferings planned from the beginning by Lucifer and his henchmen. These sufferings and torments, they were cheated from inflicting, as from the cross the Lord declared, "it is finished."

I can almost hear Lucifer screaming at God, "What do you mean it is finished? I have millions of sufferings yet to heap upon Him." Lucifer was prevented, now he and his slaves, prowl the earth seeking the Christ in those He left behind, in order to inflict those sufferings on us, while he still has some time remaining.

I stand before you a child of the Living King of the Universe, and I too bare in the witness of my scars, the wounds meant for my Lord Jesus. The scars remaining of those wounds, bare witness of the wounds meant for the Lord, and were given in an effort to belittle the call I had been given. They include the loss of the Maranatha, and all those which have been inflicted since, for the call and ministry did not end with the Maranatha.

All of this I now know was an effort of the enemy of our Lord to hurt and destroy not me, but Jesus in me, thereby inflicting great pain and suffering on our Lord. The killing of Maranatha was simply the enemy once more attempting to win the victory over Jesus the Christ of God!

Like Paul I stand honored to bare the wounds of Jesus in my body. Like my brother Paul, I too am a prisoner for Jesus, not literally imprisoned as Paul, but imprisoned by my love for Him, to be His slave. Imprisoned to stand before the enemy, declaring the victory of Calvary, even as they attempt to inflict pain and suffering upon Him through me. I am honored to stand with my brother Paul bearing the wounds of Christ as witness to the world. That my friends is the answer.

Never again when pain and suffering come our way, should we ask why the Lord or God has caused it to happen, but remember His words, "You are still in this world but you are not of it." It is the enemy, not our Lord, who in his festering unlimited hate, is pouring out pain and suffering upon the person of Jesus, through you and the Christ that lives within you. Lucifer and his minions know there is little time remaining to them and they are scrambling for a victory while they might. Bare the wounds of Christ with honor as did Paul and as do I!

You see I have traveled through life now for more than seven decades, and I have told you only a portion of my search to return to my safe place. A safe place I hold now only in one brief memory. A memory of a small child playing on the floor, in a warm loving home, on a cold Kansas Christmas morning.

In the memory the child's mother and father are seen sitting on the sofa, laughing together, as they are surrounded with the warmth of their love and the safety of their sanctuary. This memory is of Christmas 1944 and there is no warning that the tornado of my father's death will strike in just a few short weeks on January 15, 1945. When that tornado struck no one, in this family of the memory, would ever be in "Kansas" again. Our lives were changed forever.

Now, I am once again in a safe place and have been for over thirty years, since that night in a hospital in Guthrie, Oklahoma. The night when, tired of searching for a way back to my safe place, I cried out to God and He gathered me into the safety of His everlasting embrace. Now I can say with all the certainty of the ageless creation, "I ain't in Kansas no more!" I am in the safest place of all. Grace has encompassed me.

There are many stories and antidotes of Debbie's and my life aboard the S/V Maranatha yet to tell. I promise if you will join us aboard her, as we sail the Crystal Sea, you will know them all as you share with my Debbie and I the joy of the Lord's schooner——

Maranatha
"the Lord comes"
-Continued forever-

9 798890 315922